STUDIES IN ECONOMIC AND SOCIAL HISTORY

This series, specially commissioned by the Economic History Society, provides a guide to the current interpretations of the key themes of economic history and social history in which advances have recently been made or in which there has been significant debate.

Originally entitled 'Studies in Economic History', in 1974 the series had its scope extended to include topics in social history which are closely related to studies in economic history, and the new series title 'Studies in Economic and Social History' signalises this development.

The series gives readers access to the best work done, helps them to draw their own conclusions in major fields of study, and by means of the critical bibliography in each book guides them in the selection of further reading. The aim is to provide a springboard to further work rather than a set of pre-packaged conclusions or short-cuts.

ECONOMIC HISTORY SOCIETY

The Economic History Society, which numbers over 3000 members, publishes the *Economic History Review* four times a year (free to members) and holds an annual conference. Inquiries about membership should be addressed to the Assistant Secretary, Economic History Society, Peterhouse, Cambridge. Full-time students may join the Society at special rates.

STUDIES IN ECONOMIC AND SOCIAL HISTORY

Edited for the Economic History Society by M. W. Flinn

PUBLISHED

B. W. E. Alford Depression and Recovery? British Economic Growth, 1918–1939

S. D. Chapman The Cotton Industry in the Industrial Revolution

D. C. Coleman Industry in Tudor and Stuart England

P. L. Cottrell British Overseas Investment in the Nineteenth Century

Ralph Davis English Overseas Trade, 1500–1700

M. E. Falkus The Industrialisation of Russia, 1700–1914

M. W. Flinn British Population Growth, 1700–1850

J. R. Hay The Origins of the Liberal Welfare Reforms, 1906–1914

R. H. Hilton The Decline of Serfdom in Medieval England

E. L. Jones The Development of English Agriculture, 1815–1873

J. D. Marshall The Old Poor Law, 1795–1834

Alan S. Milward The Economic Effects of the Two World Wars on Britain

G. E. Mingay Enclosure and the Small Farmer in the Age of the Industrial Revolution

A. E. Musson British Trade Unions, 1800–1875

R. B. Outhwaite Inflation in Tudor and Early Stuart England

P. L. Payne British Entrepreneurship in the Nineteenth Century

Michael E. Rose The Relief of Poverty, 1834–1914

S. B. Saul The Myth of the Great Depression, 1873–1896

Arthur J. Taylor Laissez-faire and State Intervention in Nineteenth-century Britain

Peter Temin Causal Factors in American Economic Growth in the Nineteenth Century

TITLES IN PREPARATION INCLUDE

John Chartres Internal Trade in the Sixteenth and Seventeenth Centuries

R. A. Church The Great Victorian Boom, 1850–1873

F. Caron and *G. Holmes* The Performance of the French Economy, 1870–1939

Richard Johnson Education and Society, 1780–1870

J. H. S. Kent Religion and Society in the Nineteenth Century

John Lovell British Trade Unions, 1875–1933

R. Mitchison British Population Growth, 1850–1950

R. J. Morris Class and Social Structure in the Industrial Revolution

Joan Thirsk The Changing Regional Structure of English Agriculture, *c.* 1500–*c.* 1700

British Overseas Investment
in the Nineteenth Century

Prepared for
The Economic History Society by

P. L. COTTRELL

Lecturer in Economic History
in the University of Leicester

First published 1975 by
THE MACMILLAN PRESS LTD
London and Basingstoke

*Associated companies in New York Dublin
Melbourne Johannesburg and Madras*

SBN 333 13590 3

Printed in Great Britain by
THE ANCHOR PRESS LTD
Tiptree, Essex

	Acknowledgements	6
	Note on References	6
	Editor's Preface	7
	Foreword	9
1	The Volume of Capital Exports, 1815–1914	11
2	Beginnings, 1815–1855	17
	(i) The Development of the Market, 1815–1855	17
	(ii) Investment abroad, 1815–1855	19
3	The Growth of the Portfolio, 1855–1914	27
	(i) Investment abroad, 1855–1914	27
	(ii) Structural Change in the London Capital Market	30
	(iii) Two-and-a-half Long Swings in Capital Exports, 1855–1914	35
4	Capital Exports and the Borrowing Economy	41
5	Capital Exports and the British Economy	47
6	Capital Exports: The Long Swing and the Development of the World Economy	57
	Notes and References	65
	Select Bibliography	67
	Index	75

Acknowledgements

I would like to thank Professor Ford for his time and remarks, R. Rodger and Dr S. Broadbridge who both read earlier drafts, and the editor, Professor Flinn, for his help, guidance and patience. Miss Judith Watts typed the manuscript and Mr David Orme prepared the figures.

P.L.C.

Note on References

References in the text within square brackets relate to the numbered items in the Select Bibliography, followed where appropriate by the page number in italics: e.g. [4, *12–13*]. Other references in the text, numbered consecutively, relate to sources given in the Notes and References section.

Editor's Preface

RECOGNISING the need for guidance through the burgeoning and confusing literature that has grown around many of the major topics in economic and social history, the Economic History Society hopes in this series of short books to offer some help to students and teachers. The books are intended to serve as guides to current interpretations in major fields of economic and social history in which important advances have recently been made, or in which there has recently been some significant debate. Each book aims to survey recent work, to indicate the full scope of the particular problem as it has been opened up by recent scholarship, and to draw such conclusions as seem warranted, given the present state of knowledge and understanding. The authors will often be at pains to point out where, in their view, because of a lack of information or inadequate research, they believe it is premature to attempt to draw firm conclusions. While authors will not hesitate to review recent and older work critically, the books are not intended to serve as vehicles for their own specialist views: the aim is to provide a balanced summary rather than an exposition of the author's own viewpoint. Each book will include a descriptive bibliography. Above all, the aim is to help the reader to draw his own conclusions, and to guide him in the selection of further reading as a means to this end, rather than to present him with a set of pre-packaged conclusions.

M. W. FLINN
Editor

Foreword

ONE of the main factors responsible for the growth of the world economy during the nineteenth century was the flow of capital from industrial economies to the developing areas and regions. Britain was the most important creditor nation with 41 per cent of gross international investment in 1914. The accumulation of these assets is a broad subject which impinges upon, and is related to, other facets of international intercourse, especially migration and trade. A comprehensive coverage of this development is beyond the scope and size of this present essay and consequently attention will be paid only to major themes and controversies. Recent research has concentrated mainly on three topics – the measurement of the volume of capital exports, the experience of particular borrowing economies, and the relationship between the pronounced long swings in the fluctuation of foreign lending after the 1850s and the mechanism of the growth of the international economy.

1 The Volume of Capital Exports, 1815–1914

THE volume of capital exports can be estimated in two ways, directly and indirectly, and both methods have been used. The direct approach involves either measuring the total value of overseas holdings at a given point in time, producing a benchmark or stock estimate, or estimating the volume of funds subscribed to foreign security issues over a period of time. The volume of capital exports can also be derived indirectly as the residual component in the construction of balance-of-payments accounts. The two methods are liable to degrees of error and do not measure the same thing. The direct method produces estimates of gross portfolio investment and may not take into account private investment, foreign subscriptions to overseas securities floated on the British capital market, the net effect of issues made to retire existing funded or floating debt and what is confusingly known as 'direct foreign investment', for instance the private purchase by British residents of an overseas plantation. The indirect method produces estimates of net capital exports, the actual sum transmitted abroad, which includes not only subscriptions to foreign security issues but also the net balance of short-term capital exports.[1] In many respects the direct method produces estimates of what economists call *ex ante* investment, while the indirect method leads to the measurement of *ex post* investment. One of the main advantages of the direct method is that it allows the breakdown of foreign investment by geographical area and type of borrower, although its coverage may not be fully comprehensive.

Before the First World War Paish made two estimates of the value of securities and other foreign assets held by investors; the first, made in 1909, was revised in 1914 to allow for subsequent purchases. He arrived at a figure of £3714·7m. for foreign investment, which excluded investment in shipping and took 'direct investment' as being 18·5 per cent of total portfolio investment.[2] This estimate has since been adjusted by Feis [11 : 27], who considered that Paish underestimated investment in Russia and

Turkey, which when taken into account increases the 1914 total to £3763·3m.

The *Investor's Monthly Manual*, which was first published in 1865, has been used as the main source for the estimation of the annual volume of funds absorbed by overseas security issues – the other form of the direct method. This has been carried out by Hobson [21] and more recently by Simon [44], whose time series of money raised by foreign issues between 1865 and 1914 is plotted in Figure 1 (p. 14). The Simon series is more comprehensive and includes provincial as well as London issues, British subscriptions to issues made on foreign capital markets, and the private purchase of foreign securities. But coverage is not complete. The Simon estimates, as with others using the direct method, have been disaggregated in a number of ways, including the geographical composition by continent and by use of funds in terms of type of borrower. Extreme caution has to be exercised in the case of other direct estimates based upon the nominal value of securities rather than the amount of funds raised, for there was often a wide margin between the nominal value of a security and the price at which it was issued.

The indirect method was also used by Hobson [21] to produce annual estimates of overseas investment and his approach blazed a trail for subsequent estimates. Cairncross [7] has since revised downwards Hobson's series, after paying particular attention to two elements in the balance of payments, namely shipping earnings and receipts from foreign investments. This Cairncross regarded as an 'interim' revision, and in 1958 Imlah's authoritative work on the British balance of payments during the nineteenth century was published in full [22]. One of the main products was an annual series of the balance on current account from 1816 to 1914, which was the residual of eight components including visible trade, business services, emigrant funds, and tourism, and it is also plotted in Figure 1 (p. 14). Imlah considers that his series of the balance on current account, that is the net export of capital, constitutes 'a fairly close representation of British international accounts, at least for any five-year period, and it should mark more clearly and continuously the rate of growth in British foreign investments through this century' [22:*64*]. The annual estimates of Hobson, Cairncross and Imlah can be compared for the period 1870 to 1912, and there is a wide divergence between the aggregates with Imlah's estimate of £3073m., Hobson's of £2332·8m., and Cairncross's revision of the latter to £2220m. Apart from the size of Britain's international creditor position in 1870, the main reason for the divergence is the way that Hobson, Cairncross and Imlah calculated current invisible items and in particular earnings from shipping which were the largest net credits in the British balance of payments until the mid-1870s [35].

There are grounds for believing that Imlah underestimated invisible earnings from overseas-insurance business for the period 1870 to 1914. The picture presented by business histories of individual companies is of a growth of income from overseas business greatly in excess of the rate given by Imlah's data [22].[3] One further remark should be made regarding Imlah's balance-of-payments accounts for the nineteenth century. The annual balance on current account − the net export of capital − lies probably within the margin of error of his computation of the current values of imports and re-exports for the period from 1815 to 1854/5. The construction of the balance-of-payments accounts for the nineteenth century is a heroic if not herculean task and the estimates made by Hobson, Cairncross and Imlah have subsequently been widely used, but the problems and errors involved in their construction, with their consequent limitations, should be understood.

Imlah's estimates of the volume of capital exports fit closely with those produced by the direct method. Jenks [25] calculated that from 1815 to 1830 between £75m.–£88m. was invested in foreign securities and this total had risen to £195m.–£230m. by 1854. These estimates, after allowing for 'direct' investment abroad and foreign investment in Britain, following the guide lines provided by Paish, compare very well with the Imlah series of the accumulating balance abroad, namely £100·1m. between 1815 and 1829, £228·9m. for 1853, and £234·7m. for 1854. The Simon aggregate total of £3879m. for portfolio investment in 1914 agrees with Imlah's estimates and Feis's revision of Paish, after the necessary adjustments are made for the differing coverages of overseas investment. In spite of the difficulties and problems with the data series, the estimates of the volume of

13

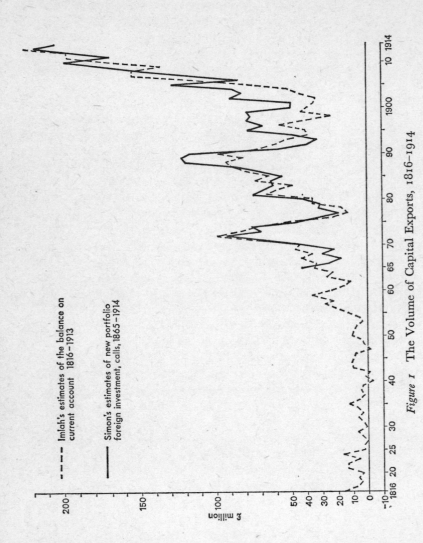

Figure 1 The Volume of Capital Exports, 1816–1914

capital exports made by both the direct and indirect methods are, surprisingly, in broad agreement, and indicate that by 1914 it amounted to approximately £4000m.

Imlah's annual series of net capital exports and Simon's series of portfolio investment can be compared from 1865 to 1913, and the two move together in the same direction in thirty-two of the forty-eight years, as can be seen in Figure 1. Both show major booms in the export of capital during the early 1870s, the 1880s, and from 1904 to 1913, with a common pattern of fluctuations of two-and-a-half long swings of thirteen to eighteen years' duration. The major dissimilarities are that the Simon series depicts a greater amplitude for the 1880s boom and an earlier recovery from the trough of the 1890s, but with a check at the turn of the century. There is also a divergence with regard to the timescape of the 1870s' boom, with the Imlah series showing a steady increase in the net export of capital during the 1860s, while the Simon portfolio data has a marked decline after the 1866 crisis. These differences are probably due to the differing coverages of the two series; the Simon data are of portfolio investment only, while the Imlah series is the net export of capital, and includes not only portfolio investment but also net short-term capital movements, net 'direct investment', the net balance of medium-term deposits placed with international banks, net private purchases of long-term securities, and changes in the ownership of existing securities as between British residents and the rest of the world.

A guide to the growth of, and the pattern of fluctuations in, the export of capital from 1815 is provided by the Imlah series. It is apparent that from 1815 to the mid-1850s the volume of capital exports was relatively low, while from 1855 there was a steady long-run growth, a change in trend which is confirmed by the Simon series. The dominant fluctuation before 1855 was the seven- to ten-year trade cycle with peaks in 1824, 1835, 1844 and 1850, and troughs in 1827, 1840, 1847 and 1853. The movement of the trade cycle is apparent after 1855 but the dominant fluctuation is now the 'long swing'. The causes of this new rhythm in capital exports are currently a major area of controversy.

2 Beginnings, 1815–1855

(i) THE DEVELOPMENT OF THE MARKET, 1815–1855

LONDON became the financial centre of the world as a result of the Napoleonic wars, which disrupted maritime trade and disorganised the commercial and financial centres of Europe established during the two previous centuries. After 1815 Amsterdam never regained its former importance, though Paris and Frankfurt-on-Main did continue to be capital markets of some standing. The main intermediaries in the London market were merchants who after 1775 became increasingly involved in the provision of international credit through dealing in bills of exchange. The demands of war finance from the 1790s gave the London mercantile community, which was being augmented by *émigrés*, experience in the flotation of debt and the remittance of subsidies to members of Pitt's coalition. Merchants and financiers were driven out of Europe by the disruption of war, and were attracted to London, which offered political stability and profitable opportunities with the rapid growth of British overseas trade. Nathan Rothschild arrived in London in 1798 from Frankfurt-on-Main, and Johann Huth came in 1809 after Napoleon's invasion of Spain.

The wartime migrants were joined by others throughout the nineteenth century, who were 'pulled' rather than 'pushed'. George Peabody, a New Englander, first came to London in 1827 to manage a branch of an American mercantile firm, but by the end of the 1830s he had established his own London house and was an important intermediary in the market for American state bonds. David and Hermann Stern of the Frankfurt Jewish banking family formed a London partnership in 1844, while their brothers became merchant bankers in Berlin and Paris, and their sisters married into the Rothschild, Bischoffsheim and Goldschmidt banking families. Family ties and trading links were not broken by the move to London, but rather formed the basis for the delicate and risky business of merchant banking.

17

Dealings in bills of exchange and the international transmission of remittances were indeed highly risky affairs. The basis for success was prudence and knowledge of the mercantile world so that doubtful bills could quickly be recognised and declined. Credit information was obtained through international networks of correspondents in which there were often filial and religious as well as business ties. Some of the most prominent mercantile and banking families were either Jewish or Huguenot, members of minority communities who had been compressed into ghettos and dispersed geographically as a result of religious persecution. Members of these groups became innovators in trade in the cities where they settled, and their prosperity was assisted by links retained with their co-religionists elsewhere, which were often reinforced by marriage. Mutual business interests provided cohesion, but individual firms within a network of correspondents did pursue differing trading policies which were conditioned by the locality of their house. This individualism meant that not all members of a merchant-banking group developed into investment bankers from being dealers in bills. Loan contracting and company promotion involved even greater risks which were not always acceptable to those who regarded prudence as the greatest virtue. In addition not all mercantile firms had either the necessary connections with government officials and representatives or subsequently sought them, preferring to continue to risk their accumulated capital in well-tried and known fields of business [29]. The transformation from a merchant to an investment banker was a slow process and many London firms retained an interest in the shipment of goods until the 1850s and 1860s. Until the 1840s the dominant investment bankers in London were Baring Brothers and N. M. Rothschild & Co., the latter having gained ascendancy in European state finance by the mid-1820s.

A new issue market for foreign securities had been established, at least in a rudimentary form, in London by the early 1820s, but a secondary market for such paper was not developed until the mid-1830s. There were limited dealings in foreign loan stock at the Royal Exchange, but the London Stock Exchange did not have a 'foreign' market until 1822 [34]. The slow growth of the secondary market in foreign securities during the first half of the nineteenth century was a direct reflection of the relatively small volume of capital exports.

(ii) INVESTMENT ABROAD, 1815–1855

Foreign lending by Britain was catholic in scope throughout the nineteenth century, but at any point of time tended to be concentrated both upon particular geographical areas, and forms of debt. After 1815 the main flow of capital went to Europe, to defeated France, and Britain's wartime allies. During the early 1820s the centre of interest switched to the newly established Latin American republics, and a speculative boom in overseas lending developed during which capital exports probably reached an overall peak for the first half of the century. In 1824 and 1825 loans of £17m. nominal for South American governments were issued and forty-six joint-stock companies, with a total nominal capital of £35m., were established to operate in the new republics. Both the issue costs and the amortisation charges on the government-debt issues were high, and none of the South American economies were able to generate sufficient foreign exchange to meet these debt-servicing charges. The result was that by the end of 1827 all the republics were in default, and only Brazil soon resumed debt payments in 1829 [38].

Most of the South American companies were speculative with twenty-eight of the forty-six being mining concerns, of which seven were Mexican. The Mexican government encouraged the participation of British entrepreneurs by tax concessions. Investors expected the introduction of the steam engine to lead to a new era of highly profitable mining, but these hopes were not realised, and by 1850 only one company of the six which actually started mining was still in existence. One example is the Real del Monte Company, whose shares of £400 with £70 paid reached a price of £1479 during the 1820s boom, but which lost £1m. between 1824 and 1844. However, the British mining companies did have some limited effect upon the Mexican industry through the introduction of new technology which was adopted by local firms [36].

The collapse of the speculative South American financial boom had a considerable effect upon the behaviour of British investors. Until the mid-1850s they turned elsewhere for investment oppor-

19

tunities. This was to be the pattern of British investment activity : a speculative spurt of lending concentrated on a particular area, followed by default and the failure of reality to match expectations. So lending turned to other areas with different lures, and the original receiving region was only able to begin borrowing again on the London market once defaults had been settled, usually by composition, and earlier disasters forgotten. Not all the funds exported during the early 1820s went to Latin America; some went to Europe, with loans to the governments of the Quadruple Alliance and finance for the formation of public utility companies.

The building of railways during the second quarter of the nineteenth century in Europe and North America gave rise to a new demand for British funds. In the 1830s railways were constructed in the eastern states of the United States, but the economy was dependent on the Old World for iron rails and finance. State governments gave aid to railway corporations in the form of assigned bonds, which were more acceptable to European investors. These securities were transferred eastward across the Atlantic along the already established financial channels of Anglo-American trade. The Atlantic mercantile houses not only retailed the bonds, initially to their personal clients and subsequently to the general public, but also were intermediaries in the transfer of railway technology. British capital was attracted to the United States for a number of reasons. In the early 1830s interest rates were higher in Boston and New York, and existing transport improvements like the Erie Canal were highly profitable. Unlike the Latin American republics, the United States Federal Debt was extinguished in 1834, while the debts of individual states at the beginning of the 1830s were small. The eastern states were wealthy and therefore the potential investor was given the impression of a credit-worthy borrower, coupled with a reasonable rate of return for his savings. Baring Brothers was the premier Anglo-American house; its rivals, with one exception, the Brown group, having either very small capitals or had only just entered the field, while N. M. Rothschild & Co. did not take an interest in American finance until 1834. Barings acted as bankers for their client states, sustaining the price of the issued bonds so as to maintain a state's London credit rating and until the early 1840s they were the sole agent for Massachusetts, Ohio, Maryland, and South Carolina [19].

American state borrowing increased rapidly after 1834 and by 1838 amounted to $172·3m., of which a quarter had been issued to aid railway development. Foreign ownership of bonds varied over time from 50 to 76 per cent, and European investors also bought securities of American banking, canal and railway companies [1]. As the volume of borrowing rose, the market in London became more competitive and speculative, with inferior securities of unascertainable maturity being sold privately and publicly by several agents with no consequent control over price. The financial crisis of 1837 had little effect on the market and borrowing reached a peak in 1838, but there is some controversy regarding the means by which this was sustained into the late 1830s in view of the partial or complete default of Arkansas, Illinois, Indiana, Mississippi, Louisiana, Maryland, Michigan, Pennsylvania and Florida in the 1840s. The flow of capital across the Atlantic during the 1840s was reversed as American securities were repatriated and this process reached a peak in 1847/8, after the British financial crisis.

American credit reached a nadir on European financial markets in the early 1840s, but conditions changed after 1847, by which time most of the states had recommended servicing their debts in full or in part. The successful conclusion of the Mexican war, the discovery of gold in California in 1849, and the collapse of the English railway mania, which led ironmasters to seek new markets for rails, were the main factors which led to investors taking up American securities again. At first they concentrated upon Federal securities issued to defray the cost of the Mexican war. Many of the older Anglo-American mercantile houses pursued a cautious policy and Barings maintained their prejudice against railway securities until 1852.

The bankers changed their attitude towards railway investment in the early 1850s as a result of their increased involvement in the Atlantic iron trade. Baring Brothers, G. Peabody & Co., and other houses started to accept railroad bonds, at first as collateral and then in direct payment for rail purchases. This led them to take securities for issue from the railroad companies or their agents [20]. Few bonds were floated publicly in London and most were bought either through stock brokers or from the merchant-banking houses. The investor was prepared to take only first-class securities, but favoured shares rather than bonds if the line was open and profitable. Securities were tailored to meet this preference with the development of first the convertible bond and then bonds secured on land grants and the railway's future earnings. With the English investor taking the 'cream', the U.S. capital markets were freed to sell more speculative paper. The American financial crisis of 1857 ended this second wave of investment, which by 1860 amounted to £100m., of which £20m. was in railroad securities, the remainder consisting predominantly of Federal debt but also including state, county and municipal bonds to aid railway development, and short-term credits [1]. British investment in the United States by the 1850s was changing in character with fewer short-term flows, as the result of the Crimean War and the 'new gold' of California, while the strategic aim of the investment was shifting from ensuring a supply of cotton to the expansion of the western granary [52].

Belgian and French railways in the 1830s and 1840s were built mainly by British contractors, engineers and navvies. French lines were financed by groups made up of English railway directors, Anglo-French bankers, Liverpool and Manchester bankers who already had an interest in domestic and American railways, and agents of various kinds [25]. These syndicates were a new financial mechanism, but did not remain distinct as various merchant-banking houses soon joined them in channelling funds into French railways. British capital also went into some European manufacturing and mining companies, but industrial firms on the continent, as in Britain, tended to be family concerns and financed internally. The British crisis of 1847, the European revolutions of 1848, and the brief British recession of 1852/3 led to the repatriation of British capital from the late 1840s, and during the 1850s French capital and contractors became the dominant force in European railway development.

The first colonial public utility company to be financed through the London capital market was a Jamaican railway company, established by members of the sugar trade during the 1840s boom. English, Scottish and Anglo-Indian mercantile houses campaigned for steam shipping services with India in the 1830s and for Indian railways in the 1840s, the East Indian Railway initially being regarded as the inland extension of the P. & O. [51]. Between 1850 and 1868 4000 miles of railway were built, which absorbed £80m. of British capital. However, only one company earned enough profits to pay a 5 per cent dividend without a state subvention, and as a result by 1869 the Indian government had paid £15m. to the railway companies under the guarantee system agreed in 1849. The other major colonial borrower before the 1860s was Canada, but the flow of capital to this country did not reach significant proportions until the 1850s with issues of state bonds to aid railway development, municipal bonds, and the securities of the Grand Trunk Railway.

Overseas portfolio investment probably amounted to about £230m. by the mid-1850s, divided geographically as shown in Table I.

TABLE I

Foreign Securities Holdings in Britain, 1854

	£m.
United States	50–60
French, Belgian, Dutch and Russian government securities	45–55
Spain and Portugal	35–45
Latin America	35–40
French Railways	25–30
Belgian railways	5
Total	195–230

Source : [25 : *13*]

The nominal value of foreign and colonial securities quoted on the London Stock Exchange in 1853 was only £31·3m. as opposed to £853·6m. of British government funds and £193·7m. of domestic railway securities [34].

Overseas investment, despite its relatively small proportions, did have, via foreign trade, an important influence upon domestic economic activity. It was estimated in 1853 that half of the European investment of £70m. in U.S. railroad securities represented financial paper obtained in return for purchases of British rails. The United States from 1847 to 1855 took between 24 per cent and 63 per cent of British exports of bar, bolt and railway iron, and this demand, stimulated by British overseas investment through the foreign-trade multiplier, had an effect upon the course of domestic income and investment.

By the 1860s a range of financial institutions had emerged in London to direct a flow of savings overseas. They ranged from merchant banks, which still retained an interest in commerce, to mining engineers and surveyors, who obtained foreign concessions in the course of their professional activities. However, a unified foreign capital market did not exist, since overseas assets and securities were obtained by investors in various ways. Securities were issued publicly through a prospectus, but a considerable proportion of savings went into paper which was sold privately and not dealt in on the London Stock Exchange. Merchant banks, ironmasters, and railway contractors took foreign railway shares and bonds in lieu of cash for the payments of debts, and these securities were unacceptable to the 'private' investors until the line was open and its profitability proved. The London market was highly imperfect in the sense that the 'private' investor was only able to buy securities which were either issued publicly or subsequently dealt in on the London or provincial stock exchanges.

While London contained the most important financial institutions which directed capital abroad, there were flows from particular regions. In 1847 forty foreign railway companies were quoted on the Liverpool Stock Exchange, the second largest group of quotations after domestic railway companies.[4] A regional analysis of the sources of capital exports is a complex task and for some types of lending is not possible because bearer securities were used. It would seem, for example, that Cornish savings, with the decline of the local mining industry from the 1850s, financed overseas mining concerns, having acquired already a knowledge of the industry and its technology. Most of the capital of the Pachua Silver Mining Company, formed in 1860 to operate in Mexico, came from Cornwall.[5] Subsequently from the 1890s Cornish capital played a major role in the development of the Malayan hydraulic tin mining industry [26].

While the various regional contributions to the flow of English capital overseas are at present almost unknown, considerable attention has been paid to the role of Scottish savings abroad, particularly with regard to the development of Australia and the United States. The main flow began after 1870, but investment contacts with these areas were established during the first half of the nineteenth century. Some Australian companies were formed in Edinburgh in the early 1820s and during the 1830s the focus of this activity shifted to Aberdeen. Initially the Aberdonian interest was in the United States, and a number of investment companies were formed on the model of the Illinois Investment Company, founded in 1837. The American state defaults shook the confidence of Scottish investors, while investment in Australia was encouraged by glowing reports from migrants. Two Australian investment companies were set up in Aberdeen though they were both weakened by the Australian crisis of 1841 to 1844. Foreign shares accounted for 15 to 34 per cent of the business on the Aberdeen Stock Echange between 1845 and 1852.[6] However, the local supply of savings was limited and in 1852/3 the Scottish Australian Company moved its headquarters to London in order to be nearer the markets for wool and capital. Before 1870 the development of jute, iron, coal and heavy engineering industries, absorbed most of the Scottish economy's savings. The second quarter of the nineteenth century, as with English overseas investment, can be regarded as an experimental phrase, during which the organisation and methods of the export of capital were established which provided the foundations for subsequent growth [33].

3 The Growth of the Portfolio, 1855–1914

(i) INVESTMENT ABROAD, 1855–1914

AFTER 1855 Britain was a substantial exporter of capital, with £4082m. being raised in London between 1865 and 1914 through the issue of foreign securities. The capital went predominantly to the temperate regions of recent settlement, this area taking 68 per cent of the 1865–1914 total, and the funds raised were used for the provision of social-overhead capital, this sector accounting for 69 per cent of the 1865–1914 aggregate, and railways alone for at least 41 per cent. With the exception of the flow to the United States, lending at any point of time was concentrated upon a limited number of borrowers, and to any area tended to take place in a single spurt. During the 1880s, for example, the main receiving regions were Argentina, Australia, and the United States, and after 1900 Canada and the United States were the predominant borrowers. Contrary to certain interpretations, there was no shift of investment after the early 1870s either to the established empire or to newly acquired colonies. The imperial share of borrowing reached a peak of 67 per cent in 1885, fell to 25 per cent during the 1890s, rose to 59 per cent in 1903 and by 1912/13 was less than 40 per cent, with the main components being Australian borrowing during the 1880s and Canadian after 1900 [44]. However, how far the regions of white recent settlement as a whole during the fifty years before 1914 constituted an informal British economic empire is a larger question.

A number of factors were responsible for the growth of overseas investment after 1855. Savings within the economy were accumulating as a result of industrialisation, but, because of the highly skewed distribution of national income, were concentrated in the hands of a small group of people. By the 1870s the number of domestic outlets for publicly mobilised savings was in certain senses declining. The railway system, in terms of its extensive geographical spread, had been completed in two waves of investment which peaked in the mid-1840s and the mid-1860s. The

27

yield on near-riskless investments, such as Consols, was falling. Manufacturing industry was organised on the basis of either the private partnership or, from the 1870s, the private limited company and, with a few exceptions, did not make use of publicly raised capital until the 1890s. Residential construction absorbed a considerable volume of savings, particularly during the mid-1870s and the 1890s, but housebuilding was financed privately and the yield on mortgages was falling. The investment policies of the insurance companies and the domestic banks, as well as of private investors, were strongly affected by the decline in yields on Consols and mortgages. This led to more adventurous attitudes, and by 1914 about 40 per cent of the funds of life offices, which in total amounted to £315m., were invested overseas. The London banks followed the pattern established by the insurance companies in the 1870s, and from the 1890s invested in an ever-widening range of foreign and colonial bonds.

The demand for capital abroad grew from the mid-1850s with railway building and the needs of financially embarrassed governments. Railway construction was a 'lumpy' investment with a long gestation period and its finance was usually beyond the capacity of locally generated savings. The need to import capital, and labour, for development was recognised by many governments, and was encouraged by guarantees of rates of return and other inducements including exclusion from local taxes.

The world economy from 1850 to 1914 has often been regarded as a very close approximation to a classical economic system. The allocation of factors of production and the distribution of goods were accordingly the result of unhindered market forces so that capital flowed internationally to where it received the highest rate of return. The gospel of economic liberalism did hold sway from the 1850s to the late 1870s but then the tide turned and ebbed so that in some respects the period breaks into two with a division in the late 1870s. During the third quarter of the nineteenth century barriers in the way of international intercourse were lowered, the most important being the reduction of tariffs on goods. Britain led the way in the inauguration of free trade, having the least to fear. U.S. tariffs were reduced from protective levels in 1846, lowered again in 1857, and with American–Canadian reciprocity, the North Atlantic was almost a free-trade area. Tariff barriers within Europe were lowered following the Cobden–Chevalier treaty of 1860. The use of 'the most favoured nation clause' developed a trading bloc which might have diverted trade as well as generating it.

International capital flows were assisted by the reform of company law and conventions which allowed corporations to straddle national boundaries. English company law was liberalised between 1855 and 1862. Shannon has analysed the limited companies registered in London, and for certain types – finance, banking, mines and land, and railway companies – has indicated whether they were formed to operate abroad. Overseas companies within these categories comprised 15·15 per cent of all companies registered and 17·18 per cent of all companies effectively formed between 1856 and 1865, excluding public halls, gas and water companies from the overall totals [43]. External flows of funds were also facilitated by the simplification of currency systems, the adoption of gold as the world monetary base, and improved communications. The gold discoveries in California and Australia increased the world's money supply, which was also augmented by the increased use of bank notes and credit. The laying of international cables knitted together the world's money markets by permitting arbitrage transactions which ironed out interest rate differentials.

The United States raised her tariff barriers at the beginning of the Civil War, but the return to protection by Western Europe did not occur until the late 1870s. Tariffs, though increased, were not raised to the levels of the inter-war years and their effect was mitigated by the fall in transport costs, the fruit of international investment. Britain, by adhering to free trade, remained a perfect creditor and sterling internationally was never in short supply because of either British capital exports or the British import surplus.

While currency systems became more unified after 1850, the world gold standard was not fully established until the 1890s. The last quarter of the nineteenth century was marked by a concern over the possible shortage of reserves, and international conferences debated inconclusively on the relative merits of gold alone and gold and silver combined. After 1873 fluctuating exchange rates, with the depreciation of silver, may have influenced the volume of British funds which went to countries on a silver standard. Investment in the Malayan tin industry, for instance, was discouraged by the continuous decline in the gold value of the Malayan silver dollar and a promotional boom in Anglo-Malayan tin companies did not begin until 1907, one year after the dollar was stabilised [26]. After the Civil War the American paper currency was an advantage to the British investors, for, although railroad securities were selling at high dollar prices in New York, they could be purchased at a discount in the undepreciated sterling [1]. The general movement back to protectionism from the late 1870s and the currency problems of the 1880s and 1890s were not totally restricting factors, but they did mould the pattern of British capital flows overseas.

(ii) STRUCTURAL CHANGE IN THE LONDON CAPITAL MARKET

The growth of capital exports from the mid-1850s led to an increase in numbers of intermediaries in the London market and the development of new forms of issuing house. The merchant banks, which increased both in size and numbers, remained the single most important group, being responsible for 37 per cent of all overseas issues between 1870 and 1914 (See Table II, p. 31). However, their market share was eroded and declined from 53 per cent, between 1870 and 1874, to 35 per cent from 1910 to 1914. New merchant banks in London were established by English provincial firms and by foreigners. During the 1850s and 1860s the merchant banker reviewed his function with respect to flotations. H. Hucks Gibbs of Antony Gibbs & Sons wrote to William, his uncle, in December 1863 :

If your theory is right, a Financial Agent is a foreign Chancellor of the Exchequer, then your whole argument is correct and a Government can't have two or more agents; but I don't think you will find the facts bear you out. Hubbards were the Russian Financial Agents, yet Barings, Hopes and Hottinguers brought out loans for them without any disturbance of the relations between the Government and their agents. . . . Governments in fact, like manufacturers, don't think it unwise to have half a dozen correspondents if need be, and see which does the best.[7]

TABLE II

Proportion of Oversea New Issues Introduced by Main Types of Issuing Houses, 1870–1914

	Official and semi-official	Merchant banks	Joint-stock banks	Overseas banks and agencies	Companies via their bankers	Other media*	Total amount issued £m.
			Percentages				
1870–4	1·8	53·0	4·4	9·6	18·2	13·0	390·6
1875–9	14·5	36·5	0·8	24·7	13·0	10·5	149·2
1880–4	6·7	38·5	3·3	14·1	26·7	19·7	355·3
1885–9	9·9	43·7	5·3	7·5	26·1	7·5	479·2
1890–4	10·4	46·4	9·0	8·8	19·6	5·8	349·6
1895–9	8·7	25·1	11·2	20·3	25·2	9·5	359·6
1900–4	27·4	19·2	17·8	14·4	16·7	4·5	258·2
1905–9	10·3	32·7	12·2	22·4	18·7	3·7	509·9
1910–14	8·3	35·2	17·4	18·8	17·5	2·8	783·8
1870–1914	9·8	37·2	10·3	15·4	20·5	6·8	
Total amount issued (£m.)	355	1354	371	562	746	248	3636

* Comprising: (a) investment trusts, £23 m., (b) finance, land and property companies, £18 m., (c) special purpose syndicates, £41 m., (d) issue houses with Stock Exchange connections, £22 m., (e) companies as their own issuers, £13 m., and (f) miscellaneous issuers, £131 m.

Source: [18:72].

This was a new, more competitive, environment. But the private family basis of the merchant bank, with its restricted resources and select clientele, limited the extent to which the house could take on new business.

This problem was first overcome by the use of groupings and syndicates, often based upon the leading bank's correspondent network and filial and religious links. The liberalisation of company law allowed a second solution, the formation of corporate investment and overseas banks, established and managed by merchant bankers but using capital subscribed by the public [28]. The 'new' bank or investment bank was only important in London during the 1860s and only one, the International Financial Society, was founded by merchant bankers, the other important concerns being formed by groups of railway financiers and contractors. More enduring were the colonial finance companies, such as the Land Mortgage Bank of India and the Australian Mercantile Land and Finance Company, which were formed to act as channels for the flow of funds to agricultural sectors abroad.

While the 'new' bank did not take hold in London as it did in Berlin and Paris, the 'Anglo-International' and 'Anglo-Imperial' banks established by merchant bankers and others during the 1860s and 1870s were in many respects 'mobilier' type banks rather than trading banks [9]. By 1870 there were seventeen international banks with branches predominantly in the Far East, South America and Europe. In 1910 there were twenty-five such banks, which had interests mainly in the Middle East and South America [3].

The decline of the market share of the merchant banks is therefore misleading, as many of the new intermediaries had been established by the merchant-banking community. Similarly, many of the investment trusts formed in London were founded by merchant bankers. The origins of some, as in the case of the Railway Share Investment Trust headed by Sir Samuel Laing and which speculated in securities and managed new issues, can be traced back to the syndicates which financed French railways in the 1840s and which in the 1860s were formalised, for a brief period, as investment banks. There was an organic growth of the London capital market with the increase in capital exports, the seed germ being the private merchant banks and railway-financing groups of the first half of the nineteenth century.

Outsiders did enter the market, particularly in the field of colonial-government borrowing, but their entry was assisted by links with the English commercial banks, which from the 1870s acted as registrars for foreign and colonial securities. In addition, the Bank of England and the Crown Agents were responsible for colonial issues. Australian states raised external loans through London issuing committees consisting of English commercial and Australian local banks and London stockbrokers. By 1914 the London and Westminster Bank, the London Joint Stock Bank, and Lloyds, together with Scottish banks, were collaborating not only with colonial banks but also with international and merchant banks in the flotation of overseas new issues. The London joint-stock banks also entered the new issue market by acting as underwriters to new issues [18].[8]

During the last decade before 1914 other London mercantile firms entered the new issue market as a result, in particular, of the growth of the rubber industry. Eastern agency houses established plantation companies and provided their protégés with local management and financial services. The plantation companies' capitals were raised both by circulating a prospectus amongst brokers and by selling securities on the Stock Exchange through the agency's broker. The agency houses acted only for the companies in which they had an interest. Some of the new mercantile issuing houses had more diverse interests: Harrison Crossfield raised capital for tea estates and tobacco firms in Java and India, Borneo timber companies and Japanese silk concerns, as well as Malayan rubber companies [46].

Alongside these institutional mechanisms, there were impermanent arrangements devised for particular issues. These normally involved the setting up of an issuing syndicate consisting probably of merchant bankers, mercantile financiers, stockbrokers, railway contractors, and mining engineers. The transitory nature of this form of floation has resulted in little information about it surviving except with respect to the Latin American government loans of the late 1860s and early 1870s, which were investigated by a parliamentary committee in 1875. *Ad hoc* arrangements were commonly used when the borrowing company or institution had neither a London banker nor a broker who could sell the securities privately. The American western mining industry was served mainly by specialist promoters in the form of mining agencies or bureaux [45].

By the mid-1870s there was a wide range of issuing houses dealing in foreign securities. They formed the primary market, floating securities in a number of ways of which the publication of a prospectus was the most common. The Stock Exchange was the secondary market, with its transactions being concerned with securities already issued, although its rules did not prevent dealings in securities before allotment. The ability to buy and sell newly created securities allowed unscrupulous company promoters and loan contractors to rig the market in the securities to which they were acting as midwives. Artificial premium creation and other dubious practices were common during financial booms and brought the London Stock Exchange into disrepute, especially during the financial depression of the late 1870s.

The secondary market did fulfil certain roles in the issue of new securities. The movement of prices was a form of thermometer of financial conditions for both issuing houses and investors. The market enabled investors to alter their portfolios but, while the length of the official list of quoted stocks was impressive, there was only an active market in a limited range of securities, particularly during financial slumps. While the Stock Exchange was essentially a secondary market, it was responsible in two respects for the introduction of securities to the London market. Both brokers and jobbers acted as arbitrageurs and, in the case of American railroad securities, arbitrage transactions were important in moving unknown shares and bonds to Britain, though their method of introduction caused some disquiet. Secondly, some broking firms developed into small merchant banks, selling privately a considerable volume of 'new' securities to their clients [1]. The London Stock Exchange was involved in a limited way in the flow of savings overseas but other countries such as France and Germany became substantial capital exporters without having such a well-developed secondary market as Britain.

(iii) TWO-AND-A-HALF LONG SWINGS IN CAPITAL EXPORTS, 1855-1914

During the second half of the nineteenth century there were three waves of overseas investment, which peaked in 1872, 1889/90, and 1913. The 1866 crisis punctuated the first upswing in lending, and the depression of the mid-1880s caused the boom of that decade to pause. It could be argued that the long swing is a mistaken description of the fluctuation in overseas lending, and instead that every other cyclical upswing tended to be stronger, so giving an impression of a long wave. The shape of the long waves was certainly asymmetrical with a long upswing to a peak, from which capital exports fell away sharply to a trough, as from 1872 to 1878. The possible causes of long waves will be left to the concluding discussion and they will be used here simply as a convenient chronology.

The first long wave had its origins in the late 1850s and can be subdivided into three shorter booms, 1855 to 1860, 1862 to 1866 and 1868/9 to 1872. The boom of the early 1870s was of considerable proportions and, while equalled during the 1880s, was not surpassed in current price values until the 1900s. Investment in the United States in the 1860s was interrupted by the Civil War and some capital was repatriated during the war. The search for alternative supplies of cotton in the Middle East and India led to an inflow of western capital into these areas, drawn by the high local rates of interest. Between 1863 and 1865 thirty-two overseas credit and finance companies, fifty international banks, and twenty-four mercantile and trading ventures were established in London – mainly to exploit the boom in raw cotton [29; 43]. Less speculative were the Australian pastoral finance companies. Capital also went to South America, in the shape of loans to governments and railway companies, and to the new nation states of southern and eastern Europe. This penetration often took place in partnership with French capital, and a number of jointly owned banks, such as the Imperial Ottoman Bank, were established as channels to convey flows of western capital.

The crisis of 1866 not only rent the London money market but also dislocated the capital market. Investors found that the new limited companies, especially the banks and finance companies, had hidden dangers and risks through high share denominations and large uncalled capitals. Lending to the United States had begun to increase after the war, but the London crisis and the financial scandal of the Atlantic and Great Western railroad, a line which had managed to obtain capital and credit from British investors and financial institutions during the war, reduced the flow [1]. Only foreign government bonds emerged from the financial upheavals of 1866 unscathed, and the low rates of interest prevalent after the crisis, as after 1857, encouraged governments with high credit ratings to approach the market.

Financial activity recovered in 1869 and lending during the 1870s boom was mainly concentrated upon the United States and Latin America. The syndicate system of loan contracting for foreign governments became firmly established at this time and was the mechanism for both public issues and the private provision of short- and medium-term bridging finance. The issue of government bonds reached an overall peak during the 1870s in terms of their share of total flotations [44]. Turkey raised a public loan on the London and Parisian markets every year from 1869 to 1874, and by the early 1870s the servicing costs involved could only be met by fresh borrowing, either publicly or privately. Peru and Egypt by the mid-1870s were also in this parlous financial position.

Purchases of American Federal bonds increased during 1869, but it was not until 1872 that the volume of railway issues, mainly of established eastern lines, reached boom proportions. Though lending declined after 1872, the London market was hardly affected by the *Krach* in Vienna in the spring of 1873 and the New York railway panic of the autumn. European rather than British investors had taken the more speculative railroad securities and consequently the London market remained receptive to American issues until the late 1870s. The American railroad market became fully developed in London during the decade with the establishment of Anglo-American banking syndicates to sell the securities. In addition, most of the houses directly entered the new issue market instead of using brokers to retail the bonds [1]. The fall in the volume of capital exports after 1872 was a response to the series of government-debt defaults, which began with Spain in 1873 and culminated in 1875–6 when Turkey, Peru and Egypt defaulted, followed by the financial difficulties of the American eastern railroad companies between 1876 and 1880.

The volume of capital exports recovered during the early 1880s and rose to a new peak in 1890. The main recipients of the funds were Argentina, Australia and the United States. Australia was the most important borrower between 1877 and 1886, taking about 50 per cent of total overseas investment in the late 1870s and 25 per cent in the 1880s. This capital went mainly into the expansion of the pastoral economy and railway construction. Australian banks and specialised pastoral finance institutions raised funds by taking medium-term deposits and issuing short-dated debentures. Railway building was financed by state-bond issues handled by local and British joint-stock banks. Government borrowing, which depended upon investment planning and the income from land sales, rose from a trough in 1873 to a peak in the mid-1880s and then remained at a high level until 1891. Pastoral borrowing was a function of the weather, and the dry period of 1881 to 1884 led to a fall in debenture issues. Scotland supplied a considerable amount of the capital which went to Australia. It has been estimated that Scottish solicitors, on behalf of clients, placed £1–2m. of new funds at the half year in bank deposits and the debentures of the land finance companies in the late 1880s, when Australian pastoral borrowing reached a peak of £5m. per annum [2; 6].

Scottish capital was also important in the flow westwards across the Atlantic. The characteristic of Scottish investment in the United States was the use of the investment trust and the land-mortgage company, financial intermediaries which had been developed in Aberdeen during the late 1830s. Four investment trusts were established in Edinburgh during the 1870s and four in Dundee, and by the end of the decade these companies had placed £4·25m. in the United States. Further trusts were formed during the 1880s together with ranching, timber and mining companies. Investment in the United States took place in two main waves, the flurry of activity of the early 1880s being halted by losses, especially in the range cattle companies and in railroad securities. A second wave of buying followed the appreciation of railroad securities between 1885 and 1887 [23]. In comparison with English capital exports, particular areas of Scotland appear to have played a wholly disproportionate role in the growth of British overseas assets after 1870. For example it has been estimated that the regional income of the Dundee textile area during the 1880s was £1·5m. per annum, but by 1890 this locality had invested at least £5m. in the United States alone [30].

By 1885 investors had switched completely out of American Federal bonds, which had bulked large during the 1870s, into railroad securities of all types. The new feature of the American railroad market in London in the 1880s was the preference for shares rather than bonds, particularly speculative shares of western lines rather than those of the established eastern companies which had been bought in the 1870s. These securities were transferred to London, especially during the early 1880s, by arbitrage transactions, but they were subsequently held by long-term investors. The market value of the British interest in American lines was about £160m. by 1881 and, following the second wave of buying between 1885 and 1887, it had increased to £300m. by the end of 1890 [1].

The other major receiver of funds during the 1880s was Argentina. The economy in 1880 had recovered from the economic and political crisis of the mid-1870s. A decade of development commenced with the inauguration of General Roca as President in November 1880, and was underpinned by his currency reform. The pacification of the pampas allowed the expansion of white settlement and agriculture, the limit of cultivation being advanced by railway construction which had begun in the 1860s. The inflow of capital into Argentina amounted to £140m. between 1885 and 1890, 35 per cent through state and municipal issues, 22 per cent for railway companies, and 24 per cent in the form of land-mortgage bonds. About £70m. was raised through flotations on the London market, while most of the land-mortgage bonds, which were sold privately, were taken by British investors [13]. Capital imports into Argentina reached a peak in 1888, by which time the rate of domestic inflation had reached a level sufficient to alarm British investors. The poor Argentinian harvest of 1889, by reducing export proceeds, foreshadowed external debt servicing problems and the political coup of the summer of 1890 was the event which caused London stock-market prices to drop sharply.

Baring Brothers had become associated with Latin America, especially Argentinian finance, since the mid-1860s. This bank first ran into liquidity problems in 1888 when an issue of Buenos Aires Water Supply and Drainage Company stock, which it had underwritten, was not taken up and a further issue in 1890 met the same fate. However, while the weakening of the market for Argentinian securities is closely associated with the autumn crisis of 1890, it would appear that Barings would have been in difficulties in any case because of mismanagement. Australian borrowing also ran into amortisation problems at the end of the 1880s because of the inadequacy of wool incomes to cover sheep stations' fixed interest obligations. A growing margin of excess capacity had developed in the pastoral industry from 1885 onwards as a result of an over-rapid expansion of output and an excessively high rate of capital formation. Yet Australian sheep farmers and British investors remained sanguine until the early 1890s, by which time a growing balance-of-payments problem had reached crisis proportions [6].

The Baring crisis resulted in a general fall in security prices on the London market, with investors selling American railroad securities in order to nurse holdings of South American stocks. Prices did recover in 1891, but this was not accompanied by a major revival of interest in the United States. Instead securities continued to be repatriated, and in 1892 the direction of the net flow of capital across the Atlantic was probably towards New York. However, the 1893 Wall Street panic did not trouble the British investor, who would appear to have brought first-class American securities at heavily depreciated prices, just as he had done after the 1873 panic. Taken together the Baring crisis, the Wall Street panic, the end of the land boom in Australia and the collapse of the banking system in 1893 were sufficient to shake confidence in all foreign securities and consequently overseas investment fell to a low ebb during the 1890s.

The impact of the Boer War upon the economy complicates the task of pinpointing the absolute trough in overseas lending after the 1889/90 peak. The estimates of Simon and Imlah diverge to such an extent in the 1890s that it suggests that short-term capital was imported between 1893 and 1899, perhaps Australian bank deposits and debentures as they matured. The little foreign investment that did take place during the decade was mainly in the speculative field of South African and Western Australian gold mining. Capital exports increased after the Boer War and rose to a massive peak by 1914, a boom which has been dubbed the 'Edwardian climax'. The amplitude of this third long wave, even after allowing for the rise in prices after 1896, was considerably greater than the two earlier waves. It was checked but not reversed by the American crisis of 1907. Although the Edwardian boom was the most massive wave of overseas investment, its causes and regional dynamics have received little attention. Lending to Canada did dominate the flow; net long-term movements of capital into the country rose from $C29·8m. in 1900 to $C47m. in 1913 but with checks in 1907 and 1912 [7]. It would appear from the data on capital imports into individual countries that investment in Argentina, Australia, New Zealand, Russia, and the United States increased sharply from 1905. During the early twentieth century, Scottish investment trusts, whose behaviour may not be typical, moved out of the land mortgage business in the United States, which was becoming less remunerative, and into securities, particularly of industrial companies rather than railroads [23]. South Africa and India were also important receiving areas, and appear to have been substantial capital importers from the 1890s.

After the 1870s railway investment was the dominant activity, but British capital also financed associated enterprises, such as milling and meat-packing, and went into other elements of transport improvement – canals, harbours, and urban tramways. Public utilities, like gas works, were also financed, as was mining. However, few funds flowed into manufacturing enterprises overseas, which between 1865 and 1914 accounted for less than 4 per cent of total subscriptions to overseas issues.

4 *Capital Exports and the Borrowing Economy*

BRITISH savings went to all parts of the world during the half century before 1914, but the largest proportion went to the temperate regions of recent settlement [44]. Therefore, the typical borrower was a relatively rich country, by contemporary standards, which was receiving not only capital from the Old World but also migrants. The imported funds went mainly into developing the infrastructure of the debtor economy. This benefited the lender by increasing the supply of raw materials but also raised land prices in the borrowing country, enriching either the private landowners or the government. Some of the borrowers, in particular the Australian states and the United States, had local capital markets. These supplied funds both to the projects, for which capital was also imported, and for urban development and land speculation, which were the consequences of the externally assisted developments. The extension of the railway network and investment in associated enterprises such as in flour-milling and meat-packing had two financial results. There were financial and wealth effects within the borrowing economy, usually the betterment of landowners. In addition the railway extended primary production, exports of which generated foreign exchange and so facilitated debt servicing.

Between 1820 and 1914 British investors supplied more long-term capital to Latin America than to any other geographical region. The major borrowing nations were Argentina, Brazil, Chile, Mexico, and Uruguay, but there were also substantial flows to Colombia, Peru, and Cuba. Capital exports to Argentina and Brazil further developed an existing export–import trading relationship. The import of capital led to economic development of an extensive nature and tended to cement, rather than overthrow, existing social structures.

The Brazilian economy contained the seed of development, but not structural change, in the expansion of coffee cultivation. This was dependent upon the construction of a railway network to link the interior with the ports. The conditions for an inflow of

41

capital were established during the 1850s and 1860s. Brazilian society contained a group of modernisers influenced by the ideals of liberalism and positivism. The country was politically stable, commercial and mercantile law was reformed, and railway construction was specifically encouraged by the state through a guarantee of a 5 per cent rate of return. By 1880 eleven British railway companies had been established to operate in Brazil. The coffee plantations remained in the hands of Brazilians, but the exporting firms, shipping companies, insurance companies and banks, as well as the railways, were either British or in the hands of other aliens.

The dominance of foreign capital over the Brazilian export sector was increased by inter-company links. English export merchants had financial interests in the shipping lines and railways, and consequently exerted pressure for better port facilities, the construction of which was financed by British capital. The bulk of the liabilities of the British-owned banks were local deposits, but they were lent primarily to the alien mercantile houses, railway companies, urban service companies, dock companies, and contractors. The majority of Brazil's imports came from Britain and were handled by English export–import houses. There was some British direct investment in textile and shoe factories, and food processing industries, but southern European migrants together with the 'new planters' of the 1870s were mainly responsible for the establishment after 1890 of local consumer goods and agricultural machinery industries. The export-orientated development of the Brazilian coffee economy had a social impact which moulded local society in a European pattern through changes in fashion, diet, styles of building, and the adoption of urban improvement. British capital exports were essentially a force responsible for the geographical spread of coffee cultivation and the facilitation of coffee exports [16].

British capital, through domination over the development of the export sector, had a similar effect upon the Argentinian economy. The landed plutocracy, though it did not invest in the new railway companies, shared a common interest with British capital in the growth of agriculture. The development of the railway system expanded the existing agrarian economy based upon large landholdings and export markets. Argentinian rail-

42

ways in 1919 were controlled by three British financial and management groups formed through interlocking directorships. The railways had substantial interests in land and mortgage companies, meat-packing, warehouses, dock companies, and urban tramways. The lines were run by British nationals, as were the associated enterprises, together with expatriate families such as the Robertsons, Parishes, Fairs, and Drabbles. The Argentinian middle classes provided local figurehead directors, but their main energies were absorbed in the professions and politics, with most ministers of public works having been at sometime a member of the legal department of a railway company [24].

The United States was the most important single borrowing nation, receiving 21 per cent of British portfolio investment between 1865 and 1914. This flow of over £835m. into the American economy did not have an impact comparable to the Latin American experience. British capital exports to the United States have been described as a 'convenience' [24]. Their share of American capital imports was of the order of 50 to 60 per cent between 1870 and 1880, but between 1869 and 1875 total net foreign investment, as a proportion of American domestic net capital formation, averaged only 15·5 per cent [52]. There is no comparable data for either Argentina or Brazil, but a comparison can be made with Australia, another primary producer with close trading ties with Britain. The net inflow of capital during the 1860s and 1870s was equivalent to 50 per cent of Australian gross domestic capital formation. Britain was the United States' major trading partner, but British goods did not dominate American imports, their share of which, by value, fell from 36·14 per cent in the period from 1869 to 1875, to 16·75 per cent in the period from 1906 to 1912.[9]

The industrialisation of the U.S. economy was the main source of the savings which financed domestic capital accumulation. However, the United States was the single most important source of foreign securities for British investors because of its size and high level of economic activity. British capital exports allowed the American economy to import rails and other capital goods which were required to supplement domestic supplies until the mid-1890s. The pro-cyclical nature of British net investment in the United States may have amplified the movement of the

American trade cycle [24]; however, it is possible that the relationship was the reverse, with the cyclical demand for capital imports originating within the U.S. economy. American railroad companies were generally locally owned or managed. British investors were suppliers of loan capital and their influence was limited to some control over access to the London capital market.

Capital inflows did give rise to a number of short-run monetary problems for the borrowing economy, in particular inflation and a balance-of-payments deficit, which in some cases checked development. Capital imports increase a debtor's national income and consequently a part in aggregate terms will be spent on consumption as well as investment. Increases in consumer expenditure will increase imports which may adversely affect the balance of trade. Inflation may result from a number of causes, including the shortage of goods and the expansion of credit. The possibility of inflation is reduced when local savings also flow into investment projects.

Capital imports also provide foreign exchange which in the short run will cover any increase in the trade deficit resulting from increased expenditure on foreign consumption and investment goods. Against this inflow of purchasing power has to be set the debt-servicing costs, which in the nineteenth century usually began from the date of the creation of the debt. Servicing charges were an unalterable burden as most issues were of fixed interest bonds rather than equity. Debt servicing was a major problem.

If capital was imported to finance investment projects which caused an increase in the volume of the debtor's exports then it augmented the flow of foreign exchange, so offsetting the debt-servicing costs. But initially there was a time lag, the gestation period of investment, during which the debtor could undergo severe balance-of-payments difficulties. In addition the magnitude of the subsequent increase in exports proceeds depended upon the type of investment undertaken and the condition of the world market for the exported goods. The price of primary products fell between the 1870s and the 1890s, but a major element in this decline was the reduction of transport costs so that the terms of trade of the primary producers were not the mirror image of those of the industrial countries. The debtor countries in the main experienced their greatest debt-servicing problems during the periods of sharp deflation in the late 1870s and early 1890s. The burden of fixed-interest debt varies with the price level, increasing during periods of deflation and becoming lighter for the borrower with inflation, the latter being the experience of Canada from 1900 to 1914.

Not all British capital exports were used to finance investment projects favourable for economic development. Many governments raised external loans to meet budget deficits. This did not lead in the long run to an improvement in the debtor's balance of trade. Some government finances, for instance those of Egypt and Turkey from the mid-1860s to the mid-1870s, were buttressed by continuous external borrowing on increasingly adverse terms. By the early 1870s these states were in a situation of having to borrow in order to repay earlier loans, with debt-servicing charges absorbing an ever-increasing proportion of state revenues. Ultimately default was the only avenue of escape, but the total effects of external borrowing were not entirely negative, for increased internal taxation did force their agricultural sectors to be more responsive to market forces and more productive.

Another view of the flow of resources from the creditor to debtor nation can be taken by comparing the stream of British overseas investment with flow of British income from abroad. Between 1856 and 1913 interest and dividends received by investors were 130·42 per cent of net foreign investment. Two inferences can be drawn: firstly, British overseas investment in aggregate was successful, and secondly, again in terms of aggregates, there was no net flow of sterling abroad as a result of capital exports; instead debt servicing exceeded net investment by 30 per cent. Using this approach, Knapp has suggested that the importance of capital exports for the economic development of the borrowing countries has been exaggerated [27]. Countries may import capital in excess of their requirements for indispensable and unrequitable foreign goods and services. 'Excess borrowing' occurs when a reduction of the liquidity preference on the part of either the banks or the public in the borrowing country, associated with a larger domestic and smaller foreign placement of securities, would not adversely affect the course of production and trade.

Rosenberg has applied this view to the position of New Zealand. Between 1840 and 1886 New Zealand had an import surplus of £44m., which was financed by £71m. of capital imports, but by 1935 the country's foreign indebtedness amounted to £225m., despite having no further import surpluses of note. Foreign borrowing did provide capital for economic development until 1887, but thereafter the foreign exchange obtained by fresh borrowing was cancelled out by interest payments, so that real savings had still to be found out of New Zealand incomes to finance the capital formation necessary for development. The need to generate export surpluses to meet interest payments, when the latter are large compared with the value of exports and imports, may retard economic growth, particularly during periods of declining export values. A borrowing economy may be forced to create the necessary export surpluses to cover debt servicing by reducing imports to below the level which corresponds to the propensity to import at full employment [39].

5 Capital Exports and the British Economy

BRITISH overseas trade and foreign investment were closely related, but the precise nature of the relationship was complicated and consequently is difficult to unravel. While changes in the levels of overseas investment and visible exports, both upwards and downwards, appear to have taken place *pari passu*, the decisions to lend abroad and to export goods were seldom taken by the same individual, and capital exports were in no way directly tied to the purchase of British goods. There is a strong correlation between the annual U.K. export of goods and the export of capital to all countries in the period from 1861 to 1914[9], but part of the strength of this statistical relationship may be the common price trend in both series. After 1870 Britain no longer had a monopoly over the world production of capital goods, and so the proceeds of loans raised in London may have been used to buy machinery, for example, from either Germany or the United States. But the increase in either American or German exports would have caused a rise in the respective country's national income, of which a small fraction may have been spent on imports from Britain.

The development of world trade on a multilateral basis from the 1850s complicates the linking mechanism between British overseas investment and exports. Before the 1890s it would appear that changes in the direction of overseas lending dampened the impact of cyclical downswings in the export demand for British goods. Saul points out that the switch of capital exports from other countries to Australia during the mid-1870s and mid-1880s increased the imperial demand for British goods, which cushioned the export trades against the full effects of the slumps of the 1870s and 1880s [40]. Similarly, any foreign orders for capital goods, as opposed to consumption goods, were unlikely to be cancelled when a boom gave way; a feature which provided British capital-goods industries with a limited buffer during a cyclical downswing. Once the multilateral system of payments became fully established during the 1890s these fortuitous factors

47

disappeared as the trade cycles of individual economies became synchronised, giving rise to a world trade cycle.

Capital exports had some effect upon British import prices. They financed the development of the primary producing countries and through improved transport facilities reduced freight charges. The consequent fall in the price of imported food-stuffs was the major factor responsible for the general increase in real wages during the last quarter of the nineteenth century. Between 1875 and 1900, as Cairncross has commented, there was 'a rare coincidence of interests' of workers and capitalists [7]. But after 1900, in spite of overseas lending on hitherto unknown scales, the cost of imported food rose and real wages either stagnated or declined.

Income from abroad was the most buoyant element in invisible earnings after 1870, and by the mid-1890s was equivalent to 43 per cent of the value of domestic exports. As a proportion of G.N.P. at market prices, net income from abroad increased from 3·48 per cent per annum average for 1870–4, to 5·98 per cent for 1890–4, and to 7·15 per cent for 1910–14.[10] Overseas income lost some of its significance for the balance of payments after 1900 with the increase in the growth, and prices,

---

Figure 2 Fluctuations, 1870–1913: key

A Subscriptions to foreign security issues: Simon's estimates of new portfolio foreign investment, calls [44].

B Ratio of the value of exports plus re-exports to retained imports: calculated from B. R. Mitchell with Phyllis Deane, *Abstract of British Historical Statistics* (Cambridge, 1971) p. 283, table 3.

C Net export of capital: Imlah's estimates of the balance on current account [22].

D Gross domestic fixed-capital formation: C. H. Feinstein, *National Income Expenditure and Output of the United Kingdom 1855–1965* (Cambridge, 1972) T. 85.

E Investment ratio; **C** and **D** as a percentage of G.N.P. calculated from [22] and Feinstein, *National Income Expenditure*, T.4 and T.85.

F Unemployment: percentage in all unions making returns: (1) 1870–92, partly computed from expenditure on unemployment benefit, (2) 1888–1913, from monthly returns of unemployment (Mitchell with Deane, *Abstract of British Historical Statistics*, p. 14).

G Rate of interest. Mean annual rate of interest on three-month bank bills, calculated from S. Nishimura, *The Decline of Inland Bills of Exchange on the London Money Market, 1855–1913* (Cambridge, 1971) table 30, pp. 117–28.

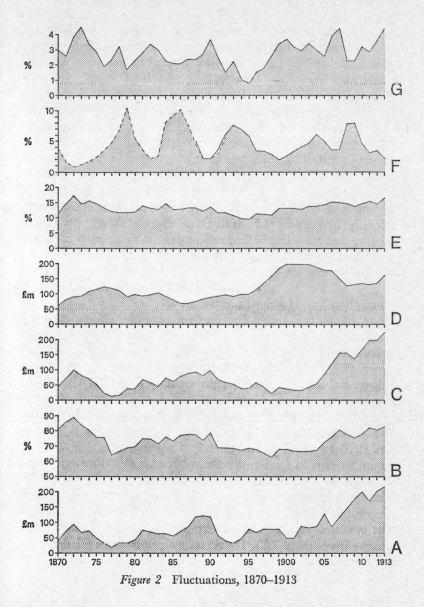

Figure 2 Fluctuations, 1870–1913

of exports. The cyclical stability of foreign income, due to the high proportion of loan capital in overseas investment, offset the downswings in export proceeds during slumps. If equities had made up more of Britain's foreign assets, then overseas earnings would have had a more pro-cyclical nature and consequently would have been less stable in the long term.

Interest and dividends from abroad became the largest net credit item in invisible earnings during the 1870s. The process of foreign investment after 1875 has often been regarded as the passive reinvestment of foreign earnings in the manner of a revolving fund. This view has been challenged by Ford who has pointed out that income from abroad entered the domestic income stream in the same way as any other income and so could be spent or saved in any desired way. It was not earmarked simply for foreign investment [12]. If this is so, why did Britain not experience any strain on her balance of payments as a result of booms in overseas lending? This question involves two problems: the relationship between foreign investment and the export of goods, an issue which has already been raised; and, the interaction between home and foreign investment.

In the analysis made by Ford a possible deficit situation caused by overseas lending was removed by an improvement in the balance of trade, with export values expanding relatively to imports (**B**)*. The increase in export values was due to foreign lending. Subscriptions to foreign security issues (**A**) increased the borrowing countries' national incomes, a fraction of which was spent on imports from Britain, and this improved the British balance of trade. According to Ford's calculation for the period from 1870 to 1914, approximately 75 per cent of the current-account surplus in foreign-investment booms over that prevailing in troughs is attributable to relative increases in export values, assuming that imports remain unaltered. The Ford thesis therefore proposes a strong link between fluctuations in foreign security issues (**A**); the ratio of export to import values (**B**); and overseas investment (**C**). It receives support from Tinbergen's study of the late Victorian economy, which found a positive net association between capital exports and the short-term rate

* References in round brackets refer to the plots in Figure 2, p. 49.

of interest (**G**), implying that funds did become scarce within the economy during booms in overseas lending [5].

The increase in export values during periods of high lending was not cancelled out by rising domestic incomes drawing in more imports for three reasons. Firstly, an increase in export values would only bring about an equivalent increase in imports, through the mechanism of the foreign-trade multiplier, if the marginal propensity to save was zero. Secondly, Ford maintains that investors did forgo current consumption in order to buy foreign securities. Thirdly, in the long run there was an inverse relationship between home and foreign investment so that the income generating effect of increased export sales was offset by a decline in domestic investment (**D**).

One of the features of the post-1870 economy is the long-run inversity of home and foreign investment. It was first pointed out by Cairncross [7], who found that the movement of the terms of trade failed to explain the timing of booms in foreign investment before 1900. While the terms of trade moved against Britain from 1873 to 1881, foreign lending did not increase until 1878, and during the 1880s boom in capital exports the terms of trade were favourable. Subsequent investigations have also found that the terms of trade, in a direct way, are a poor explanatory variable of fluctuations in overseas investment. In an examination of the flow of capital to Australia, Canada, the United States, New Zealand, and Argentina, Richardson, using multiple-regression techniques, found that the terms of trade, as an explanatory variable, were only significant in the case of Australia and Canada but with a positive sign in the case of Australia and a negative sign with regard to the flow to Canada [37]. Thomas has argued with considerable strength that the real significance of the terms of trade lies not in the ratio of export to import prices but in the quantities – factor movements, volumes of exports and imports, and rates of productivity – implicit in the terms of trade [49].

Thomas maintains that at the crest of each long wave in overseas lending the terms of trade moved sharply in Britain's favour as a result of rapid appreciation of export prices, the event at the core of Ford's thesis. However, whereas Ford places stress on the primacy of lending, Thomas attributes the appreciation of export prices to the short-run inelastic nature of the supply

51

curves of the capital-goods industries. In Thomas's view the movements of the terms of trade were a consequence of, rather than a causal factor determining, the long-run inversity of home and foreign investment.

While home and foreign investment were out of phase in the long run, they appeared to move together in the short run. With the exception of the 1890s home boom, increases in foreign investment pulled the economy out of slumps between 1870 and 1914. The link between foreign lending and the general revival of economic activity was the export sector, with a boom in overseas investment causing a rise in the demand for exports. Incomes within the export sector consequently increased and new investment took place when capacity began to be fully utilised. The rise in incomes and investment led to demands for domestic goods and services, and a general economic revival ensued [7]. Cairncross's explanation of the workings of the foreign-trade multiplier, as with Ford's thesis regarding the transfer of foreign investment, places considerable stress on the pivotal role of overseas lending. The Cairncross model of the behaviour of home and foreign investment has been reappraised by a number of people. Bloomfield has found that home and foreign investment not only moved inversely in the long run between 1860 and 1914 but also in the short run [4]. Stone, in trying to assess the impact of a financial panic in the London capital market upon the foreign/domestic mix of total investment from 1880 to 1913, has also statistically tested the model proposed by Cairncross [48].

Stone found that the volume of domestic investment was determined by the growth of national income, wage rates, the terms of trade, orders for capital goods, and interest rates. Foreign investment was correlated positively with the growth of national income and interest receipts from abroad and negatively with the terms of trade. However, the Cairncross model was found to be incomplete, this being suggested by the non-random nature of the errors in the statistical relationships. The hypothesis that in the short run foreign and home investment moved together was improved by the insertion of dummy variables to represent the panics of 1890 and 1907. This not only removed autocorrelation from the statistical equations, but also revealed that the terms of trade were a poor explanatory variable of domestic

52

investment except in panic years. The effect of the two crises was a reduction in both home and foreign investment for the following four years.

Cairncross regarded home and foreign investment as being drawn from a common pool of savings, but the total investment rate (E), the sum of domestic and overseas investment as a proportion of G.N.P., does fluctuate between 1870 and 1914.[11] It was at its highest level (17·21 per cent) in 1872, but did rise rapidly after 1903 to 16·55 per cent in 1913. Its movement appears to be strongly influenced by fluctuations in foreign investment, with the average rates for 1881–9 and 1904–13 being 13·15 per cent and 15·2 per cent respectively, while the rate during the domestic boom of the 1890s was only 11·38 per cent (1891–8 average). The rate is only an impression because of imperfect data, but two alternative inferences can be drawn from its trend. Firstly, during booms in overseas investment the propensity to save increased, or, and more pessimistically, the domestic economy was unable to absorb productively the savings generated by it, so that during booms in home investment investors either increased their consumption, and/or their investment portfolios became more liquid.

The trend of employment appears possibly to have been inverse to the movement of overseas lending. Trend-rises in foreign investment were found by Ford [14] to be associated with trend-rises in unemployment (F). It is possible that the growth of exports during foreign-lending booms was an insufficient generator of economic activity to compensate for the effects of the fall in domestic investment. Caution has to be exercised because of our lack of knowledge concerning unemployment during this period. Its apparent higher level during periods of capital exports has been explained by Brown [5] on the grounds that the transfer of foreign lending was under-affected, resulting in gold losses. The loss of monetary reserves led to an increase in interest rates (G) which depressed both home and foreign investment, so causing a higher level of unemployment. The main contrast is between the 1880s and the 1890s, with the boom in foreign lending during the former decade taking place possibly against a background of higher unemployment. In the early 1870s and after 1905, when similar booms in overseas investment occurred, interest rates rose but unemployment did not increase. One conclusion is that exports were less competitive in the 1880s, and this is supported by the ratio of export to import values (B), being 75·5 per cent average for 1885–9, as opposed to 84·1 per cent for 1870–4, and 80·2 per cent for 1910–13.

One of the major criticisms of the late Victorian economy is that too much was invested abroad, to the detriment of domestic economic growth [32]. It is argued that the institutions of the London capital market were biased towards making large foreign issues, so starving British industry of the finance that it required for new investment projects. This statement has to be looked at in a number of ways. Firstly, large flotations were less costly to make on the London market. Securities in some volume were required for an active secondary market on the Stock Exchange. Most domestic industrial share issues before 1890 were of relatively small size, with the result that the London market was unattractive to industrialists because of the cost of raising capital. In addition investors did not like small issues because the secondary market in them was 'thin'. Edelstein has attempted to see if investors were biased in any way in their choice of securities. Using econometric methods, a weak and unstable preference for large foreign issues was revealed for the period 1870 to 1889. Between 1890 and 1914 there was a less unstable bias for domestic issues and a continuing, though very weak, bias for large issues [10]. Secondly, there was little contact between London issuing houses and industrialists. Most merchant bankers had *émigré* origins and had a greater knowledge of conditions overseas than in the Midlands and the North. However, too much stress can be placed on the problems of access to the London market. While an examination of the London Stock Exchange List in 1913 shows that quoted domestic industrial securities amounted to only £873m., a mere 8 per cent of the total nominal value of quoted securities, an unfavourable inference ignores the methods by which industry raised finance.

It is difficult to generalise, but the representative manufacturing concern was a family-based unit, organised either as a partnership or a private limited company. Its financial needs were met by the plough-back of profits, bank loans, and trade credit. There was a strong resistance to raising capital externally particularly equity, for this would dilute the family's control over its concern. While the title 'the age of steel and electricity' is often applied to the period after 1880, the onset of increased financial demands, caused by the introduction of capital intensive production processes, varied between industries. In ship-building it became pronounced from the 1890s with the development of electric, hydraulic, and pneumatic power transmission and the availability of a new range of machine tools, but some industries remained labour-intensive until 1914.

McCloskey [32] has looked at the general effects of a possible excess of capital exports as a part of an attempt to assess the growth potential of the late Victorian economy. Critics of the debilitating effects of capital exports have pointed out that, from 1911 to 1913, the return on domestic physical capital was 10·7 per cent, while on foreign bonds it was only 4·7 per cent. McCloskey argues that possibly some of this yield gap is accounted for not by differing qualities of investment, private equity capital at home and loan capital abroad, but was due to the bias of the market in favour of foreign issues. The counterfactual that McCloskey explores is the removal of this imperfection and its effect upon domestic growth. The removal of the greatest market imperfection between 1870 and 1913 would have required 'enormous capital *imports*' but would have only increased the rate of growth of income from 2·4 per cent to 2·58 per cent per annum. Capital exports, in McCloskey's view, were therefore not a possible surplus on which the economy could have drawn for growth, but his approach ignores what the effect of an increase in domestic investment would have had upon the structure of the post-1870 economy. It is doubtful whether McCloskey's firm conclusions will have brought the debate to a close. The subject is not simply the reallocation of savings between domestic and foreign outlets but includes also the role of banks in the finance of industry and the motivation of the late Victorian business unit.

6 Capital Exports: The Long Swing and the Development of the World Economy

LONG-SWING fluctuations of about eighteen years are apparent in capital exports from the late 1850s, and become noticeable in domestic investment from the mid-1870s. Emigration from Europe to North America, and American building and railroad investment also display long swings which are in harmony with those present in British capital exports, but are inverse to the swings in British domestic investment, particularly in building. Those long swings in various economic and demographic variables reveal possibly the rhythm of the economic growth of the Atlantic community, a major segment of the world economy. After 1850 the international movement of factors of production and goods was almost unfettered and, given this high degree of integration of the world economy, the analysis of capital movements can be conducted in terms of the strength of domestic and foreign opportunities in the form of varying degrees of push and pull. Such an analysis can also be applied to emigration. The source of current controversy is the extent of interaction between components of the world economy and whether international forces resulted in the inversity of the long swings in British home and foreign investment.

At the centre of the debate is the Atlantic economy thesis propounded by Brinley Thomas [50]. After a major study of nineteenth-century trans-Atlantic migration, Thomas concluded that there was a rhythm of growth produced by a population-determined investment cycle of about eighteen years. The Atlantic economy was a closed system in which phases of infrastructure investment alternated between the debtor/migrant-receiving economy and the creditor/source-of-migrants economy. Initially the relationship explored was between the United States on the one hand and the United Kingdom with continental Europe on the other, but the Atlantic system has since been expanded to include Canada, Argentina and Australia, the other main areas of recent settlement.

The process of growth was the extensive exploitation of new sources of primary products in the 'periphery' of the economy which required supplies of capital and labour from the 'core'. The phases of population-sensitive capital formation see-sawed between the periphery and the core, providing new increments of export capacity. The upper turning points of phases of growth were brought about by monetary instability, but the alternating bouts of infra-structure investment, with the whole periphery undergoing simultaneously long swings in capital formation inverse to those of the core, were the result, in Thomas's model, of inverse demographic cycles.

The presence of simultaneous long swings can be used as the criterion to delimit the constituent economies of Thomas's periphery. This investigation has been carried out by Bloomfield in a study of the patterns of fluctuation in international investment [4]. The Canadian economy, which was influenced strongly by its southern neighbour, was a part of the periphery of the Atlantic economy. The turning points of long swings in Canadian net capital imports, gross immigration, urban building, communications construction, and G.N.P. are broadly similar to American and inverse to the swing pattern of British domestic investment and building. The long-swing pattern in the Australian case differs from the Atlantic formulation, with falls in capital imports and immigration in the late 1860s and early 1870s, and, conversely, increases during the mid- and late 1870s. The 'Atlantic'/Australian experience is difficult to substantiate, and at best can be summarised as only one-and-a-half long swings from 1860 to 1913, with the turning points in the case of capital imports being 1885 (peak) and 1907 (trough). Argentinian data are scanty, and available series reveal two spurts of lending/ migration – one in the 1880s and a second after 1905. There would appear to be no overall swing, though Ford concludes that British investment in Argentina between 1880 and 1914 'exhibited long swings roughly similar to long swings in total British overseas investment but opposite to British domestic investment' with the rider that 'bursts of lending were particularly concentrated' [15]. From this it would appear that the periphery of the Atlantic economy consisted only of the United States with Canada and Argentina. Australia, in spite of its heavy dependence upon British capital and labour, followed a different growth path, the parameters of which during the 1880s and after 1907 give a semblance of an 'Atlantic' orientation.

The criticisms of the Thomas 'Atlantic' economy have tended to concentrate on the degree of push–pull reaction between the American and British economies, particularly with regard to the inverse relationship of building. While Habakkuk [17] is prepared to accept a long swing in American building activity from the beginning of the nineteenth century, he maintains that British building before the 1870s followed a seven/ten-year cycle. It cannot be disputed that building booms in the United States and Britain from the 1870s alternate, but Habakkuk lays stress on domestic factors, far removed from the 'Atlantic' economy, as being responsible for the generation of long swings in British building from the mid-1870s. He accepts that migration could have caused the British building cycle to have had an inverse relationship with the American, but the variations in the emigration rate compared with the growth of population were too small to have had this influence.

Long swings in British building were, in Habakkuk's view, the result of the financial maturity of the economy after 1870. The absence of 'commercial panics' during the last quarter of the nineteenth century both changed the nature of the supply of capital to the building industry and altered the demand for housing. During financial slumps investors switched to lending on mortgage, which ensured the supply of finance for building, especially during the mid-1870s and early 1890s. In addition effective demand was no longer disrupted by decennial monetary crises. In this interpretation 'Atlantic' push–pull factors were only of any major importance during the 1880s – an exceptional decade in the sense that there was during it a constant external demand for capital and migrants. But, although funds were pulled abroad, this did not result in a shortage of finance for domestic building. The depressive influence upon the course of domestic building was, instead, the conjunction of the foreign demand for labour together with the weak state of the domestic economy. Migrants were pushed, as well as pulled, abroad by the depression of arable agriculture, the severe industrial slumps of the late 1870s and mid-1880s, and the very weak recovery of the

59

early 1880s. 'This is the clearest case of emigration at the expense of urbanization' [17].

Thomas lays stress upon the rhythm of growth of the Atlantic economy as being a product of interaction between the core and periphery. Another view can be taken of the generation of long swings in which they are the result of the influence of the American economy through trade as well as factor flows. Williamson [52] has analysed the British balance of payments, exploring two possible hypotheses: firstly, that the American economy created its own increasing supply of capital during domestic booms through American demand having a major determining influence upon the rate of growth of British exports, and hence the size of the British balance of trade; secondly, that the prices of American exported grain and cotton had a smoothing effect upon the value over time of total British imports.

Using data from Imlah, Williamson found mild long swings in British deflated import values after 1850, their presence in current price values being masked by the contrary movement of import prices. The long swing in deflated imports after 1870 moved in harmony with the swing in British domestic investment. The movement of British import prices was found to be the result of supply conditions affecting American production of cotton and grain, especially before 1860. Long swings were more apparent in deflated exports than in deflated imports and begin in the late 1840s, a decade earlier. A major causal factor was variations in American demand for imports. Swings in deflated British exports moved directly with swings in U.S. imports from the 1840s, and the secular fluctuation in the two series becomes closely matched from the 1860s.

Therefore it is highly possible that the well-established long swings in American output, income and investment were imprinted upon the British economy through induced fluctuations in British exports and marginally through the cost of American cotton and grain imports. What is debatable is the strength of this transmission mechanism after the 1870s. The main market for British exports was Europe, which was both larger and more stable than the United States. American demand declined from the 1880s and its cyclical volatility was offset by the greater stability of both European and imperial demand. The

60

full development of multilateral trade by the 1890s had the effect of synchronising cyclical trading fluctuations. In addition, by the late 1900s changes in the American demand for British goods had little effect upon the British economy and, overall, upon the rest of the world economy [41].

Williamson found long swings in the British balance of trade from the 1860s and, unlike the secular movements of imports and exports, they are similar to the American pattern, with the balance of trade deteriorating during domestic booms. The trade balance in periods of overseas lending, as Ford suggests, improved as a result of the expansion of export values rather than because of a reduction in import values.

Long swings are most obvious in the fluctuation of capital exports, and there is a strong similarity in their timing and pattern with the secular swing in American capital imports. However, the American demand for capital only had a strong influence upon the fluctuation of the volume of British capital exports between 1860 and 1880. Some other influence has to be sought for the continuance of long swings in British capital exports after 1880. The decline of the strength of the Anglo-American linkage during the last quarter of the nineteenth century also makes more problematical the continuance of inverse American and British building cycles.

The possible long-swing generators are Argentina from the 1880s and Canada after 1900. Such an interpretation stresses the primacy of the periphery rather than long swings being the result of interaction within an 'Atlantic' system. The long swing in capital exports to Argentina has been examined by Ford [15]. This country between 1880 and 1914 received about 8 per cent of total British overseas portfolio investment but few British migrants. The timing of lending appears to have been determined by the rate of profit on existing Argentinian railways, a pull factor, and the general receptiveness of the London capital market to new overseas issues. The influence of domestic British investment in claiming or releasing savings was found to have been weak.

The long swing enters the relationship through both total British overseas new issues and the Argentinian railway profit rate. The latter displays a fifteen-year cycle which is possibly a result of both real and financial factors, namely the gestation period of railway investment and the speculative 'spurt' nature of British overseas investment. The long gestation period of infrastructure investment, together with the population structure, are responsible for the lags in the Thomas 'Atlantic' model. Ford proposes the chronology for the railway development cycle shown in Table III.

TABLE III

Railway Development Cycle

Years	
1–5	Influx of foreign funds, railway construction begins
6	Financial crisis
4–8	Completion of new lines
7–11	Traffic builds up to reach existing network capacity
9 onwards	Profits of railway companies increase
10–14	Preconditions established for a new spurt of borrowing

This form of a railway building induced long swing has a general applicability. With the exception of the United States, single speculative spurts of lending were a characteristic of British overseas investment in the temperate primary producers from the 1860s to 1914. Most lending was in the form of fixed interest securities, the servicing of which usually resulted in the capital importer experiencing balance-of-payments difficulties during the gestation period of the investment project. The new lines extended the area of commercial export-orientated agriculture. As output rose, freight traffic built up,and the railway companies' profits increased. This made their securities more attractive to British investors. With favourable world prices for the exported produce, the balance of payments of the capital importer improved, providing the foreign exchange for the resumption of debt servicing on externally held securities.

Argentina shared with North America some common factors influencing the growth of their respective economies. These were the world market conditions for primary products, particularly cereals and later meat, and the general receptiveness of the

London capital market to foreign new issues. The two factors in one way were connected since British investors, by the late 1870s, understood the relationship between the price of American railroad securities and the volume of cereal shipments on the American railway network.

For five years, the painful process of foreclosure settlement, and reorganisation was steadily going on, and in 1877 and 1878 the railroads were greatly assisted by the heavy tonnage arising from the large crops, until at length in 1879, the idea dawned upon investors, speculators, and capitalists that the railroads were not really the worthless properties that they had seemed to be. Then there was a rush to purchase low-priced stocks and bonds such as never had been seen before, and the advance in price was marvellous.[12]

Railways absorbed at least 41 per cent, possibly as much as 44 per cent, of the funds subscribed to overseas new issues made on the London market between 1865 and 1914. The amplitude of the railway-investment long swing was greater because attached to the purchase of railway securities was the parallel finance by British investors of allied activities such as the provision of land mortgages, food-processing, warehousing and dock construction. The profit rate on these activities moved probably in harmony with the railway profit rate. This long swing was not directly related to migration, but railway-building did also allow the extension of settlement, both urban and rural. However, it had no direct connection with the British domestic-building cycle, except tenuously through the receptiveness of investors to foreign securities.

The gestation period of the investment and the build-up to capacity levels are factors which shape the long swing but it is difficult to isolate any general elements responsible for the initiation of the railway cycle. In the case of Argentina the pacification of the pampas, political stability, and Roca's currency reform would appear to have paved the way for the inflow of funds during the 1880s. A recent study by Richardson [37] shows that British funds and migrants were pulled rather than pushed abroad. It was found that factor flows were demand-determined, with an expanding national income in a potential borrower economy inducing an increase in investment and then, as domestic savings were insufficient, external sources of finance were attracted. This analysis, as with those related to the Atlantic economy, looked at the areas of recent settlement which in aggregate took about 68 per cent of British portfolio overseas investment between 1865 and 1914. The other components of British overseas investment have received little attention. Investment in Europe until the mid-1870s and after 1907 was substantial and there was an important flow to Africa between 1900 and 1905, and from the mid-1890s until 1914 Asia took on average £19·08m per annum of British funds. While the mechanism behind the rhythm of British investment in the areas of recent settlement is still far from clear, the role of capital exports to Africa, Asia, and Europe has yet to be closely investigated.

Notes and References

In the Notes and References and the Select Bibliography the place of publication is London, unless otherwise stated. The abbreviation *E.H.R.* represents the *Economic History Review*.

1. See A. I. Bloomfield, *Short-term Capital Movements under the pre-1914 Gold Standard* (Princeton, N.J., 1963); and P. H. Lindert, *Key Currencies and Gold* (Princeton, N.J., 1969).
2. G. Paish, 'Great Britain's Investments in Other Lands', *Journal of the Royal Statistical Society*, LXXI (1909) 456–80; and *The Statist* (14 Feb 1914) Supplement, pp. *v–vi*.
3. See also B. Supple, *The Royal Exchange Assurance* (1970) pp. 214–15, 241–51.
4. J. R. Killick and W. A. Thomas, 'The Provincial Stock Exchanges, 1830–1870', *E.H.R.*, 2nd series, XXIII (1970) 105.
5. Public Record Office, London: File BT 31/483/1904.
6. R. C. Michie, 'The Scottish Stock Exchanges in the Nineteenth Century', mimeographed research paper presented to the Economic History Conference (Bristol, 1974) p. 1.
7. Guildhall Library, London: papers of A. Gibbs & Sons, merchant bankers; H. H. Gibbs's Private Letter Book, vol. III, MS. 11036/3 – letter to William Gibbs, 4 Dec 1863.
8. C. A. E. Goodhart, *The Business of Banking, 1891–1914* (1972) pp. 138–41.
9. Calculated from *Historical Statistics of the United States, Colonial Times to 1957* (Bureau of the Census, Washington, D.C., 1960) pp. 552–3, series U134–151.
10. Calculated from C. H. Feinstein, *National Income Expenditure and Output of the United Kingdom, 1855–1965* (Cambridge, 1972) table 10.
11. Calculated from ibid., and Imlah [25], with total investment being regarded as the sum of gross domestic capital formation and the balance on the current account.
12. *Commercial History and Review of 1880*, p. 5, supplement to *The Economist* (1881).

Select Bibliography

[1] D. H. Adler; M. E. Hidy (ed.), *British Investment in American Railways, 1834–1898* (Charlottesville, 1970). A major study of the growth of British investment in a very important area. See also [19, 20, 23, 24, 45, 52].

[2] J. D. Bailey, 'Australian Borrowing in Scotland in the Nineteenth Century', *E.H.R.*, 2nd ser., XII (1959–60). Reveals the importance of Scottish savings, channelled through the medium of solicitors, in the flow of capital to Australia in the 1880s. See also [6, 18, 33].

[3] A. S. J. Baster, *The International Banks* (1935). An important survey of the activities of the 'Anglo-International' banks. See also D. Joslin, *A Century of Banking in Latin America* (1963) and [8].

[4] A. I. Bloomfield, *Patterns of Fluctuation in International Investment before 1914*, Princeton Studies in International Finance, no. 21 (Princeton, N.J., 1968). A survey of overseas investment with particular stress upon long swings and their causation.

[5] A. J. Brown, 'Britain and the World Economy', in *Studies in the British Economy, 1870–1914*, ed. J. Saville, Special Number, *Yorkshire Bulletin of Economic and Social Research*, XVII (1965). A general article which contains a critique of [14].

[6] N. G. Butlin, *Investment in Australian Economic Development 1861–1900* (Cambridge, 1964). Should be read in conjunction with his earlier statistical work, *Australian Domestic Product, Investment and Foreign Borrowing, 1861–1938/9* (Cambridge, 1962). Stresses domestic factors as being responsible for the flow of funds to the southern continent, an interpretation at odds with [50]: on Australia see also [18].

[7] A. K. Cairncross, *Home and Foreign Investment 1870–1913* (Cambridge, 1953). The various estimates have been replaced by [22 and 44] and C. H. Feinstein, *National Income, Expenditure, and Output of the United Kingdom 1855–1965* (Cambridge, 1972). The explanation of the alternation of home and foreign investment booms has been modified by [4 and 48]; and the author has entered, since, a rather inconclusive debate over the role of the London capital market as a provider of funds

for domestic industry – see A. R. Hall, 'A Note on the English Capital Market as a Source of Funds for Home Investment before 1914', *Economica*, n.s., XXIV (1957), and A. K. Cairncross, 'The English Capital Market before 1914 – A Reply', *Economica*, n.s., XXV (1958). However, the monograph remains a major study of British investment and its fluctuations during the late Victorian period.

[8] P. L. Cottrell, 'London Financiers and Austria 1863–1875; the Anglo-Austrian Bank', *Business History*, XI (1969). A case-study of the formation and early activities of an 'Anglo-International' bank. See also [3].

[9] J. H. Dunning, *Studies in International Investment* (1970). See especially 'Introduction' on the difference between portfolio and direct investment, and chapter 4 'British Investment in the United States 1860/1913'.

[10] M. Edelstein, 'Rigidity and Bias in the British Capital Market, 1870–1913', in *Essays on a Mature Economy; Britain after 1840*, ed. D. N. McCloskey. Examines the efficiency of the London capital market and attempts to establish, by econometric techniques, the preferences of investors. See also [32 and 42].

[11] H. Feis, *Europe the World's Banker, 1870–1914* (New York, 1930, reprinted 1965). A survey of European foreign investment and its relationship to international politics; contains a revision of the Paish estimates of British overseas assets in 1914.

[12] A. G. Ford, 'The Transfer of British Foreign Lending 1870–1913', *E.H.R.*, 2nd ser., XI (1958–9). Takes a Keynesian approach to the transfer problem, arguing that new foreign issues, by expanding export values relatively to import values, augmented substantially the current account surplus; criticises [22] and earlier work.

[13] A. G. Ford, *The Gold Standard, 1880–1914; Britain and Argentina* (Oxford, 1962). A study of Anglo-Argentinian relations. See also [15, 24, 31] and H. S. Ferns, *Britain and Argentina in the Nineteenth Century* (Oxford, 1960).

[14] A. G. Ford, 'Overseas Lending and Internal Fluctuations 1870–1914', in *Studies in the British Economy, 1870–1914*, ed. J. Saville, Special Number, *Yorkshire Bulletin of Economic and Social Research*, XVII (1965): reprinted in A. R. Hall (ed.), *The Export of Capital from Britain, 1870–1914* (1968). Continues the analysis begun in [12] and shows a possible relationship between the trend in unemployment, and upswings in foreign

investment, but on this point see [5]. See also A. G. Ford, 'Notes on the Role of Exports in British Economic Fluctuations, 1870–1914', *E.H.R.*, 2nd ser., xvi (1963–4).

[15] A. G. Ford, 'British Investment in Argentina and Long Swings, 1880–1914', *Journal of Economic History*, xxxi (1971); reprinted in R. Floud (ed.), *Essays in Quantitative Economic History* (Oxford, 1974). Suggests that the long swing in investment in Argentina may be the result of the interaction between Argentinian exports and railway building.

[16] R. Graham, *Britain and the Onset of Modernisation in Brazil, 1850–1914* (Cambridge, 1968). Examines the impact of foreign investment upon the Brazilian economy. See also [24].

[17] H. J. Habakkuk, 'Fluctuations in House-Building in Britain and the United States', *Journal of Economic History*, xii (1962); reprinted in A. R. Hall (ed.), *The Export of Capital from Britain, 1870–1914* (1968). A major article which gives a different interpretation to [50] by stressing the role of domestic influences in the alternation of British and American building cycles after 1866. See also S. B. Saul, 'House Building in England, 1890–1914', *E.H.R.*, 2nd ser., xv (1962–3), and E. M. Sigsworth and J. Blackman, 'The Home Boom of the 1890s', in *Studies in the British Economy, 1870–1914*, ed. J. Saville, Special Number, *Yorkshire Bulletin of Economic and Social Research*, xvii (1965).

[18] A. R. Hall, *The London Capital Market and Australia 1870–1914* (Canberra, 1963). An important monograph, which contains both an extremely useful survey of the development of the London capital market and an analysis of the flow of capital to Australia. See also [6].

[19] R. W. Hidy, *The House of Baring in American Trade and Finance* (Cambridge, Mass., 1949). The only detailed monograph by a business historian of a major London merchant bank. Unfortunately its scope is restricted to the bank's American activities and the history ends in 1860. See also A. J. Murray, *Home from the Hill* (1971), which is a general account of the development of F. Huth & Co., and [28 and 29].

[20] R. W. Hidy and M. E. Hidy, 'Anglo-American Bankers and the Railroads of the Old Northwest, 1848–1860', *Business History Review*, xxxiv (1960). Provides an account of the change in function, from merchant to banker, of the Anglo-American houses during the 1850s. See also [1], and R. W. Hidy, 'The Organisation and Functions of Anglo-American

Merchant Bankers, 1815–1860', *Journal of Economic History*, I, supplement (1941).

[21] C. K. Hobson, *The Export of Capital* (1914; 1963, with a preface by Sir R. Harrod). A classic study but now statistically out of date.

[22] A. H. Imlah, *Economic Elements in the Pax Britannica* (Cambridge, Mass., 1958; reprinted New York, 1971). The only source of annual estimates of net overseas investment throughout the nineteenth century, but see [35 and 41].

[23] W. T. Jackson, *The Enterprising Scot; Investors in the American West after 1873* (Edinburgh, 1968). A very lucid monograph, which traces the flow of Scottish savings across the Atlantic.

[24] L. H. Jenks, 'Britain and American Railway Development', *Journal of Economic History*, XI (1951). An extremely important article which surveys the role of British capital in the construction of the railway network in both Argentina and the United States. It maintains that British capital only aided and abetted existing trends within the social structures of the economies. See also [16 and 51].

[25] L. H. Jenks, *The Migration of British Capital to 1875*, 2nd ed. (1963). A pioneer work, which in parts is factually incorrect, but as yet is still unsurpassed.

[26] W. L. Ken, *The Malayan Tin Industry to 1914* (Tucson, 1965). A useful regional study. See also [46].

[27] J. Knapp, 'Capital Exports and Growth', *Economic Journal*, LXVII (1957). A theoretical and empirical article, which seeks to minimise the role played by capital exports in the growth of the developing countries during the nineteenth century. See also [39]; J. D. Gould, *Economic Growth in History* (1972) chapter 3 (C); and H. B. Chenery and A. M. Strout, 'Foreign Assistance and Economic Development', *American Economic Review*, LVI (1966).

[28] D. S. Landes, 'The Old Bank and the New; the Financial Revolution of the Nineteenth Century', *Revue d'histoire moderne et contemporaine*, III (1956); translated and reprinted in F. Crouzet *et al.* (eds), *Essays in European Economic History 1789–1914* (1969). Traces the evolution of the corporate investment bank, drawing mainly on the French experience, but has considerable relevance. One section of the footnotes provides a critical bibliography for the early development of the London market, to which should be added K. F. Helleiner, *The Imperial Loans* (Oxford, 1965).

[29] D. S. Landes, *Bankers and Pashas* (1958). A brilliant account of the western economic penetration of Egypt in the 1860s, with extremely useful general chapters concerned with the development of investment banking in Europe, and the London capital market in the 1860s.

[30] B. Lenman and K. Donaldson, 'Partners' Incomes, Investment and Diversification in the Scottish Linen Area, 1850–1921', *Business History*, XIII (1971). A local analysis of the factors which led to the export of Scottish capital and its consequent effects upon the domestic economy.

[31] C. Lewis, 'Problems of Railway Development in Argentina, 1857–1890', *Inter-American Economic Affairs*, XXII (1968). Stresses the importance of political factors.

[32] D. N. McCloskey, 'Did Victorian Britain Fail?', *Economic History Review*, 2nd ser., XXIII (1970), has as one of its themes the refutation of the argument that overseas investment was a source of savings which could have been drawn upon to promote domestic economic growth. McCloskey's analysis has been examined by W. P. Kennedy, 'Foreign Investment, Trade and Growth in the United Kingdom 1873–1913', *Explorations in Economic History*, XI (1974), who concludes that the growth potential of the economy was restricted by the way savings were deployed. It should be noted that this number of *Explorations in Economic History* contains other relevant papers presented to the Anglo-American Conference on British Economic History, 1973, which had as its theme 'Britain in the World's Economy 1860–1914'.

[33] D. S. Macmillan, 'Scottish Enterprise in Australia 1789–1879', in *Studies in Scottish Business History*, ed. P. L. Payne (1967). An account of the origins of the economic links between Scotland and Australia. See also D. S. Macmillan, *Scotland and Australia, 1788–1850; Emigration, Commerce and Investment* (Oxford, 1967).

[34] E. V. Morgan and W. A. Thomas, *The Stock Exchange, Its History and Functions*, 2nd ed. (1971). The standard history of the London Stock Exchange. See also W. A. Thomas, *The Provincial Stock Exchanges* (1973).

[35] D. North and A. Heston, 'The Estimation of Shipping Earnings in Historical Studies of the Balance of Payments', *Canadian Journal of Economics and Political Science*, XXVI (1960). A critical survey, which includes coverage of [7, 21, 22], concerned with the methods used to estimate shipping receipts.

[36] A. W. Randall, *Real del Monte: A British Mining Venture in*

71

Mexico (1972). A business history of one of the companies formed during the 1820s boom.

[37] H. W. Richardson, 'British Emigration and Overseas Investment 1870–1914', *E.H.R.*, 2nd ser., xxv (1972). An econometric investigation of the determinants of the flow of labour and capital to the areas of recent settlement. The statistical results favour a demand-pull type of explanation. See also [4].

[38] J. F. Rippy, *British Investments in Latin America 1822–1949* (Minneapolis, 1959). A source of benchmark statistics of investment in South America *but* in terms of *nominal* values. See also [44 and 47].

[39] W. Rosenberg, 'Capital Imports and Growth – The case of New Zealand – Foreign Investment in New Zealand, 1840–1958', *Economic Journal*, LXXI (1961). An application of the Knapp approach [27] to the New Zealand case.

[40] S. B. Saul, *Studies in British Overseas Trade, 1870–1914* (Liverpool, 1960). A collection of important essays: see especially chapter IV 'The Pattern of Settlements: II The Export of Capital', and chapter V 'Trends and Fluctuations'.

[41] S. B. Saul, 'The Export Economy', in *Studies in the British Economy, 1870–1914*, ed. J. Saville, Special Number, *Yorkshire Bulletin of Economic and Social Research*, XVII (1965). A valuable general survey article, which contains some criticism of Imlah's estimates of invisible earnings [22] and of the 'Atlantic Economy' thesis with respect to trade in goods.

[42] J. Saville, 'Some Retarding Factors in the British Economy before 1914', *Yorkshire Bulletin of Economic and Social Research*, XIII (1961). An article which contains a useful summary of the argument that the London capital market was biased towards overseas investment. See also [7, 10, 18, 32, 43] and D. S. Landes, 'The Structure of Enterprise in the Nineteenth Century. The Cases of Britain and Germany', *XIe Congrès international des sciences historiques, Rapports*, v, *Histoire contemporarie* (Uppsala, 1960).

[43] H. A. Shannon, 'The First Five Thousand Limited Companies and their Duration', *Economic History*, II (1929), and 'The Limited Companies of 1866–1883', *E.H.R.*, VIII (1933); reprinted in E. Carus Wilson (ed.), *Essays in Economic History*, I (1954). A very useful source of information on early companies, but unfortunately the statistics are in terms of the number of companies formed rather than the capital raised.

[44] M. Simon, 'The Pattern of New British Portfolio Foreign

Investment, 1865–1914', in *Capital Movements and Economic Development*, ed. J. H. Adler (1967); reprinted in A. R. Hall (ed.), *The Export of Capital From Britain* (1968). A statistical article, which is the only source of data on subscriptions to new foreign issues – *ex ante* foreign lending. The series is disaggregated by geographical area and by type of borrower, with some limited analysis and interpretation of the findings.

[45] C. C. Spence, *British Investments and the American Mining Frontier 1860–1901* (Ithaca, N.Y., 1958). An illuminating case study which should be read in conjunction with [1]. See also [23].

[46] R. T. Stillson, 'The Financing of Malayan Rubber, 1905–1923', *E.H.R.*, 2nd ser., xxiv (1971). An example of investment in the tropics. See also [30].

[47] I. Stone, 'British Long-term Investment in Latin America, 1865–1913', *Business History Review*, xlii (1968). Replaces [38] but again is only in terms of *nominal* values, so the estimates of [44] are preferable.

[48] J. M. Stone, 'Financial Panics: Their Implications for the Mix of Domestic and Foreign Investments of Great Britain, 1880–1913', *Quarterly Journal of Economics*, lxxv (1971). Despite its title, says very little about the impact of financial panics, but does test the Cairncross model of investment behaviour and finds it wanting in some respects. See also [4].

[49] Brinley Thomas, 'The Historical Record of International Capital Movements to 1913', in *Capital Movements and Economic Development*, ed. J. H. Adler (1967), reprinted in Brinley Thomas, *Migration and Urban Development* (1972). A survey of estimates of foreign investment with an analysis of its determinants. It argues that the movement of the terms of trade is a consequence, rather than a cause, of the alternation of savings between domestic and foreign outlets.

[50] Brinley Thomas, *Migration and Economic Growth: A Study of Great Britain and the Atlantic Economy*, 2nd ed. (Cambridge, 1973). A major but controversial study which lays great stress upon migration and population growth as being the determinants of investment. See also [7 and 17]; Brinley Thomas, *Migration and Urban Development* (1972); E. W. Cooney, 'Capital Exports and Investment in Building in Britain and the United States', *Economica*, n.s., xvi (1949), and 'Long Waves in Building in the British Economy of the Nineteenth

Century', *E.H.R.*, 2nd ser., XIII (1960); and J. Parry Lewis, *Building Cycles and Britain's Growth* (1965).

[51] D. Thorner, *Investment in Empire, British Railway and Steam Shipping Enterprise in India 1825–1844* (Philadelphia, 1950). An account of the Anglo-Indian mercantile community's campaign for improved communications. See also D. Thorner, 'Great Britain and the Development of India's Railways', *Journal of Economic History*, XI (1951), a provocative article, which concludes that the introduction of the railway did transform the Indian economy but the change was from traditional to modern backwardness.

[52] J. G. Williamson, *American Growth and the Balance of Payments 1820–1913* (Chapel Hill, N.C., 1964). See especially chapter VI which is an analysis of long swings in Britain's international accounts. An earlier version 'The Long Swing: Comparisons and Interactions between British and American Balance of Payments, 1820–1913', *Journal of Economic History*, XXII (1962) has been reprinted in A. R. Hall (ed.), *The Export of Capital from Britain 1870–1914* (1968).

Index

Aberdeen   25, 37
Aberdeen Stock Exchange   25
agency house   33
Amsterdam   17
arbitrage transactions   29, 34,
    38
Argentina   27, 37, 38–9, 40,
    41, 42–3, 51, 57, 58, 61–4
Atlantic and Great Western
    Railroad   36
Atlantic economy   57–64
Australia   25, 27, 31, 35, 37,
    39, 40, 41, 43, 47, 51, 57,
    58–9
Australian Mercantile Land and
    Finance Company   32

balance of payments   11, 12,
    48, 50
  balance on current account
    12, 45
  deficit   44, 62
  receipts from foreign invest-
    ment   12, 45
  shipping earnings   12, 13
balance of trade   44, 50, 60,
    61
Bank of England   33
banks
  commercial   28, 33, 37, 55
  international   32, 41
  investment   32
  merchant   17–18, 24, 30–3

Baring Brothers   18, 20–1, 30,
    39
Belgium   22, 23
Berlin   32
bill of exchange   17, 18
Bischoffsheim family   17
Bloomfield, A. I.   52, 58
Boer War   39–40
bonds   20, 24, 36, 38
  convertible   22
  fixed interest   44
  land-mortgage   38
  railroad   21, 36, 38
  state   21–2, 23, 37
Brazil   19, 41–2
Brown, A. J.   53
Buenos Aires Water Supply
    and Drainage Company
    39
building cycles   59, 61, 63
building industry   59

Cairncross, A. K.   12, 13, 48,
    51–3
Canada   23, 27, 28, 40, 45,
    51, 57, 58, 61
capital exports
  and British import prices   48
  estimation   11–13
  fluctuations in   14–15, 27,
    35, 43–4, 47–53, 56–64
  and foreign trade   23,
    47–51, 60–1

capital exports–*cont.*
  from Cornwall   24
  from Scotland   25, 37–8, 40
  short-term   11, 15
  stock estimate   11
  and unemployment   53–4
  See also overseas investment
Civil War   29, 35–6
Cobden–Chevalier treaty   29
coffee   41–2
company promotoin   18, 33,
    34, 35
Consols   28
cotton   35, 60
Crimean War   22
crises
  1837   21
  1847   21, 22
  1857   22, 36
  1866   15, 35, 36, 59
  American crisis of 1907   40,
    52–3
  Australian crisis of 1841 – 45
  Baring crisis of 1890   39,
    52–3
Crown Agents   33

debenture   37, 40
debt servicing   39, 41, 44–6
default   37, 45
deflation   45
demographic cycles   58
direct foreign investment   11, 15
domestic economy   54–5, 59
domestic investment   24,
    27–8, 51–5, 61
  fluctuations in   27, 51–3,
    58–61
Dundee   37–8

East Indian Railway   23
economic development   41
Edelstein, M.   54
Edinburgh   25, 37
Egypt   36, 37, 45
emigration   25, 41, 57–8, 59,
    61, 63
Erie Canal   20
excess borrowing   45

Feis, H.   11, 13
finance companies   31, 35, 36
Ford, A. G.   50–3, 58, 61–2
foreign exchange   44, 46
foreign-trade multiplier   24,
    51, 52
France   19, 23, 34, 35
Frankfurt-on-Main   17

Germany   34, 47
Gibbs, Antony, & Sons   30
Gibbs, H. Hucks   30
gold standard   29
Goldschmidt family   17
Grand Trunk Railway   23

Habakkuk, H. K.   59
Harrison & Crossfield   33
Hobson, C. K.   12, 13
Holland   23
housebuilding   28, 57, 59
  American   57, 58, 59, 61
  British   58, 59, 61
  Canadian   58
Huguenots   18
Huth, J.   17

Illinois Investment Company
    25

Imlah, A. H.   12–15, 39, 60
Imperial Ottoman Bank   35
income from abroad   45,
    48–9, 50
industrial finance   54–5
inflation   38, 44
insurance companies   28, 41
interest rates   20, 35, 53
    and domestic investment   52
    short-term   50–1
international banks   32
International Financial Society
    32
investment bank   32
investment banking   18
investment company   25
investment trusts   31, 32, 37, 40
Investor's Monthly Manual   12
invisible earnings   13, 45, 48–9

Jenks, L. H.   13
Jews   18

Knapp, J.   45–6

Laing, Sir S.   32
Land Mortgage Bank of India
    32
land-mortgage bond   38
land-mortgage company   37,
    40, 43
limited company   28, 29, 35–6
Liverpool Stock Exchange   24
loan contracting   18, 30, 33, 36
London   17, 18, 24, 25, 27,
    28, 30–4, 35, 39, 44, 47,
    52, 54, 61
London Stock Exchange   18,
    23, 24, 31, 34, 39, 54

'long swing'   15, 35, 51–2,
    56–64

McCloskey, D. N.   55
Malaya   24, 33
marginal propensity to save
    51
merchant banking   17–18, 24,
    30–3, 54
Mexico   19, 24, 41
mortgage   28

Napoleonic wars   17
national income   27, 44, 52,
    64
net capital exports   11, 12, 15
new issue market   18, 30–3
New York   20, 36, 39
New Zealand   40, 46, 51

overseas investment
    in 1854   23
    in 1914   11–12, 15
    in Africa   64
    in Argentina   27, 38–9, 40,
        41, 42–3, 51, 58, 61–4
    in Asia   64
    in Australia   25, 27, 33, 35,
        37, 39, 40, 43, 47, 51,
        58–9
    in Belgium   22, 23
    in Brazil   41–2
    in Canada   23, 27, 40, 51,
        58, 61
    in Egypt   36, 37
    in the Empire   27
    in Europe   64
    in France   19, 22, 23
    in Holland   23

overseas investment–*cont.*
  in India   23, 35, 40
  in Latin America   19–20, 23,
      27, 33, 35, 36, 38–9, 40,
      41–3
  in Malaya   24, 33
  in the Middle East   35
  in mining   19, 22, 24, 34, 40
  in New Zealand   40, 46, 51
  in Peru   37, 41
  in Portugal   23
  in Russia   11, 23, 40
  in South Africa   40
  in southern and eastern
      Europe   35
  in Spain   23, 37
  in Turkey,   12, 36, 37
  in the United States   20–2,
      23, 25, 27, 34, 36, 37–8,
      39, 40, 43–4, 51, 58
  See also capital exports

Pachua Silver Mining Company
    24
Paish, G.   11, 13
Paris   17, 32
Peabody, G.   17
Peabody, G., & Co.   21
Peninsular & Oriental Steam
    Navigation Company
    (P. & O.)   23
Peru   36, 37, 41
plantation companies   33
portfolio investment   11, 13,
    15, 23
Portugal   23
primary products   44–5, 62–3
propensity to import   46
propensity to save   53

prospectus   34

railway contractor   22, 24,
    32, 33
railway development cycle
    62–3
Railway Share Investment
    Trust   32
railways   20–3, 24, 27, 28, 35,
    36, 37, 38, 40, 41, 61–4
  American   20–1, 22, 34, 36,
      37, 38, 40, 44, 57, 63
  Argentinian   42–3, 61–4
  Belgian   22, 23
  Brazilian   41–2
  French   22, 23
  Indian   23
  Jamaican   32
range cattle companies   37
Real del Monte Company   19
real wages   48
Richardson, H. W.   51, 63
Roca, General   38, 63
Rosenberg, W.   46
Rothschild family   17
Rothschild, N.   17
Rothschild, N. M., & Co.   18,
    20
Royal Exchange   18
rubber industry   33
Russia   11, 23, 30, 40

Saul, S. B.   47
savings   27, 61, 64
Scottish Australian Company
    25
secondary market   18, 34, 54
Shannon, H. A.   29
shares   24, 38

ship-building industry 55
short-term capital exports 11,
    15, 22
Simon, M. 12, 13, 14, 15, 39
solicitors 37
South Africa 40
Spain 23, 37
Stern, H. 17
Stone, J. M. 52–3
syndicate 22, 32, 33, 36

terms of trade 44, 51–2
Thomas, B. 51–2, 57–60, 62
Tinbergen, J. 50
trade cycle 15, 35, 44, 47–8,
    50, 59
transport costs 44

Turkey 12, 36, 37, 45

unemployment 53–4
United States 20–2, 25, 27,
    28, 29, 34, 35, 36, 37–8,
    39, 40, 41, 43–4, 47, 51,
    57, 58, 59–60
United States Federal Debt 20
    21, 22, 23, 36, 38

Vienna 36

wage rates 52
Wall Street 39
Williamson, J. G. 60–1
world economy 28–9, 56–64
world trade 47–8